T0294443

Patterns of Deprivation in the Soviet Union Under Brezhnev and Gorbachev

Patterns of Deprivation in the Soviet Union Under Brezhnev and Gorbachev

Mervyn Matthews

Hoover Institution Press, Stanford University

Stanford, California

Hoover Press Publication 383

First printing, 1989

Manufactured in the United States of America

95 94 93 92 91 90 89   9 8 7 6 5 4 3 2 1

Library of Congress Cataloging-in-Publication Data

Matthews, Mervyn.
    Patterns of deprivation in the Soviet Union under
Brezhnev and Gorbachev / Mervyn Matthews.
          p.   cm. — (Hoover Press publication)
    Bibliography: p.
    Includes index.
    ISBN 0-8179-8831-9. —
    ISBN 0-8179-8832-7 (pbk.)
    1. Poor—Soviet Union.   2. Soviet Union—
Economic conditions—1965–1975.   3. Soviet
Union—Economic conditions—1976–
4. Soviet Union—Social conditions—1945–
5. Cost and standard of living—Soviet
Union.   I. Title.
HC340.P6M378   1989   89-32392
362.5'0947—dc20   CIP

To Mila, Owen, and Emily

Contents

1 | Gorbachev's Social Policies
Current Problems of Public Well-Being

2 | Soviet Living Standards and Consumer Reactions
Measures of Shortage, Expectation, and Satisfaction

Tables

Acknowledgments

I am indebted to many friends and colleagues for help over the long gestation that this book has required. Perhaps the best order of acknowledgment is chronological, although it does not accord with the sequence of the studies presented here. In 1982, the National Council for Soviet and East European Research in Washington, D.C., provided the bulk of the funding for a survey of Soviet emigré families. I wish, in particular, to thank Dr. Vladimir Toumanoff, Dr. Blair Ruble, and Professors Vlad Treml, Gregory Grossman, and Bernice Madison for the support and advice they offered at that time.

I collected further material at the Russian Research Center, Harvard University, during my tenure of a Mellon Fellowship there. I would like to express my gratitude to the director, Professor Adam Ulam, and other fellows for providing congenial working conditions and access to Harvard's excellent libraries. More useful research was done, in this and other spheres, during a summer session at the Hoover Institution on War, Revolution and Peace at Stanford University. I wish to thank Dr. Richard F. Staar, senior fellow, and Mr. Robert Conquest, senior research fellow of the Institution, for making my research possible. The first draft of the present work was written while I was a visiting professor in the Department of History, University of Western Ontario. I owe a particular debt of gratitude to Professors Robert Hohner and Charles Ruud of that department.

Despite all the pressures on British academics, certain of my colleagues at the University of Surrey have given me the maximum support possible. I am grateful to the Research Committee and the Department of Linguistics and International Studies for their support, some vital funding, and their generally helpful attitude.

The list is long, but I must add several names more. The first is that of

Priscilla MacMillan, whose unbounded kindness allowed me to solve some locational problems near Harvard Square. In England, Miss Tamara Romanyk and Dr. Vladimir Moss helped with text-inputting and transliteration. At the Hoover Institution Press, Mr. Raymond Meyer edited the text with exemplary care and retuned parts of it for the American ear.

Preface

At the time of the 1917 Revolution, Russia was a relatively poor peasant land. One of the principal aims of the Bolshevik leadership was to transform her into a highly industrialized community, free and untainted by exploitation. The application of Marxist doctrine would ensure an egalitarian distribution of the wealth produced by willing hands, while socialist planning would make the country the envy of the capitalist world.

Seven decades have passed since the Bolsheviks came to power, but Soviet society is still poorer than the capitalist West and not very egalitarian, either. Alas, much of the history of the USSR may be thought of in terms of social catastrophe—war, famine, poverty, heartless administration, and militaristic expansion. Only after the death of Stalin in 1953 did a more humanitarian spirit prevail and the well-being of the people receive due attention. Even so, in the matter of raising living standards and eradicating poverty a great distance still remains to be traversed. In *Poverty in the Soviet Union* (p. 27), I have estimated that at the beginning of the 1980s up to two-fifths of the population lived below a recognized, and quite low, poverty line.

The study of material well-being in the Soviet Union, however, presented great difficulties for several decades. Soviet economics and sociology, the disciplines most closely involved in such an investigation, have long been fettered by the taut exigencies of state secrecy. Statistics on family income and related subjects have been collected—indeed, in large quantities—but few have been published. Words like "poor" and "slum" were banned in official literature as descriptions of any social group or condition. Among Western observers, many excellent minds have addressed the problem of analyzing the Soviet economy. Yet, perhaps not surprisingly, their attention centered on the broader questions of national growth, average standards, and how far the USSR lags behind capitalist states. Against this background the social aspects of deficits of consumer goods, relative deprivation, and poverty in general have been rather neglected.

Looking behind the veil of secrecy, which is only now beginning to be lifted, we find the response of the Soviet authorities to poverty-related matters to be somewhat curious. The official stance has been that differences in earnings are popularly approved and fair. Since the state ultimately controls investment policy, most wage systems, the occupation structure, and the supply of consumer goods and services, one might argue that the poverty engendered by low pay and shortage of goods and services is, to a degree, tolerated by the state. Low levels of support for pensioners and those who cannot earn, or cannot earn enough, are also part of a deliberate policy. In terms of simple theory there is little to stop the Soviet government from standardizing wages and rations for every soul in the land. This admirably egalitarian step has, of course, never been taken and never will, because it would destroy the whole system of socioeconomic incentives. Poverty in the Soviet Union thus has a certain inbuilt inevitability and, like poverty elsewhere, can only be removed by piecemeal measures.

I have felt for some time that many aspects of Soviet poverty were not being adequately monitored, even by observers who purported to do so.* Several years ago, however, concern about the shortcomings of the study of Soviet poverty prompted me to sketch out a possible framework for more coherent investigation. I wanted to move beyond economics and to undertake a broader, more socially oriented analysis. My work was facilitated by a tentative investigation of "minimum" budgets under Khrushchev that had—surprisingly—resulted in the publication of reasoned Soviet criteria for determining poverty thresholds. True, the figures covered only small urban families and were in some respects unreliable. But since such families made up a large part of the Soviet population, a degree of cautious generalization was possible. The figures were accorded little publicity in the USSR, because when set against average earnings, they implied that a majority of Soviet citizens lived in poverty. Public discussion of so shameful a matter could not be encouraged. However, some of the data provided allowed me to explore the social implications of poverty in the Soviet Union.[1]

The material on deprivation and poverty presented here is new, and in

---

* An example of such inadequacy is Alastair McAuley's book *Economic Welfare in the Soviet Union* (1979), which (astonishing though it may now seem) virtually ignored the influence of the second economy and the real value of benefits obtained by the elite through administrative channels. Western scholarship has in recent years tended to adopt a more comprehensive approach.

our view its presentation needs little justification. The subject is important and so vast as to make its study practically endless: as a result of Gorbachev's policies, official materials are again becoming more easily available, and the copious unofficial data are still inadequately researched. The leadership's far-reaching plans for reform need analysis from this angle, too.

The studies that make up this volume are intended to take the story firmly forward into the late 1980s. The first of them endeavors to summarize M. S. Gorbachev's more important social policies and assess their effect. Of course, at the time of writing, there is no guarantee that the Soviet leader will be able to complete his programs, nor any certainty that, if completed, these programs will assuage old evils. It seems clear, however, that he favors a harsher economic climate, with more social differentiation and less protection for inefficiency. Although economic advances must, in the end, benefit everyone, many of his policies do not augur well for the less privileged in Soviet society.

Next I present an overview of Soviet studies of a relatively new topic in Soviet sociology, namely, popular levels of expectation regarding the satisfaction of material needs and wants and the degree to which these expectations are satisfied. Data of this kind, when set against assessments of ideal levels of provisioning, or the levels achieved, provide some rather specific measures of relative deprivation and of popular reactions to it. Much of this work predates Gorbachev's advent to power.

The third study in this volume is an edited version of a report, submitted to the U.S. National Council for Soviet and East European Research, on 348 families who emigrated from the USSR, and who were "poor" before they did so. Such interviews were one way of compensating for the impossibility of sociological investigation in the country itself. The questionnaire used in the study bore on certain central elements in the respondents' life-styles and on attitudes common among them. Though necessarily limited in scope, the survey provided, I believe, some rather original insights into practices and attitudes common in the USSR in the late 1970s and early 1980s. The text has been somewhat shortened and amended to include some unused material from the original data banks.[2]

The last study is intended to illustrate another much-commented-upon aspect of Gorbachev's policies: *glasnost'*, or openness in the press. This openness has already been found to have marked limitations, but fortunately for us it has permitted the public discussion, to an extent hitherto impossible, of social ills. The articles I have chosen for consideration include scholarly analysis of poverty-related problems and personal accounts of poverty describing plights that must be common. The texts have been abridged and paraphrased where necessary for purposes of comment and analysis.

I hope that the material presented in this book will not only improve understanding of the USSR but also encourage further, and possibly more revealing, research. The present time is one of rapid change—or attempted change—and writing about it is not easy. I would be grateful for the reader's indulgence if some of my conclusions are in fact overtaken by events. May I say, in conclusion, that although great care has gone into the treatment of facts and ideas, error is unlikely to be entirely absent from the following pages. For any that may come to light, the author assumes full responsibility.

1 | Gorbachev's Social Policies

Current Problems of Public Well-Being

Introduction

All Soviet leaderships since the days of Stalin have recognized the need to raise the living standards of the people and make Soviet society a better place to live in. Since assuming the general-secretaryship of the CPSU in March 1985, Mikhail Sergeevich Gorbachev, together with his closest associates, has proclaimed similar aims and made strenuous efforts to promote them. My object in the first part of this study is to review the main social policies enunciated during his first three years or so of office and such consequences as have made themselves apparent. Every decade or so, the Soviet Union seems to undergo a kind of sociopolitical spasm that unsettles or reverses the achievements of the governments that preceded it. So was it with Stalin, Khrushchev, and, to some extent, Brezhnev. The social changes that Gorbachev is trying to effect are, if anything, even more profound than those sought by his predecessors and are thoroughly deserving of analysis.

The situation he inherited has already been much commented upon. There is no doubt that Soviet living standards had stagnated and in some ways fallen since the late 1970s. The consumer continued to suffer from severe shortages of goods and services, while being showered with propaganda about socialist well-being. Public dissatisfaction with the state of affairs was, it would seem, intense. In a broader sense the economy was over-administered, inefficient, and provided people with no incentive to work harder. Indiscipline and alcoholism were so common that Iurii Andropov, whose protégé Gorbachev was, felt obliged to start a national campaign against them.

Most of the social ills are hard to quantify, since the censorship long prevented the publication of relevant data and inhibited public discussion. Yet, when Gorbachev took office, in most respects the country remained far from its socialist ideals. Soviet living standards were still, according to reliable foreign estimates, a third (or less) of those of the United States—its chosen rival—and the gap was probably widening.[1] Soviet social problems, despite their specificity, much resembled those of well-developed bourgeois countries and in some ways were more acute. Solving them—insofar as social problems can be "solved"—must be a long-term task. Furthermore, the Soviet leader's utterances have been replete with references to internal opposition, and such opposition has been stubborn at all levels, from the Politburo down to the localities.[2]

Consideration of present developments in the USSR must take into account not only the government's attempted solutions but also the popular response to them, especially when a forceful personality like Gorbachev calls for fundamentally new attitudes in the work force and, indeed, in society as a whole. Innovative legislation may be proclaimed in the pages of the central press, only to be undermined by obdurate resistance in the apparatus and by popular dislike. Analysis of the situation is complicated by the extent and profundity of the proposed changes, which Gorbachev himself described as *perestroika*—"reconstruction"—and even as "revolution."

My approach is fairly simple and may be outlined as follows: After examining the provisions of the current five-year plan for improving living standards in general, I look at Gorbachev's proposals in the sphere of incentives. This topic raises the knotty problems of distribution of rewards, egalitarianism, and the role of the proposed private sector. Gorbachev seems to have adopted a rather original policy toward employment, particularly insofar as it concerns the individual toiler.* Here we need to examine the matter of job security and discipline, which have far-reaching social implications. Next I consider new provisions for the visibly poor sections of the community, especially respecting pensions and state grants. This discussion is followed by an examination of recent policy toward the long-suffering Soviet village and by a concluding note on the so-called democratization campaign. The effect of *glasnost'* deserves, I feel, a section in its own right.

There is no doubt that many other current policies are relevant to social

---

* *Toiler* (*rabotnik, trudiashchiisia*) is used here as the superordinate category encompassing workers, employees, and peasants. A worker (*rabochii*) does manual labor or is engaged in industrial production. A peasant (*krestianin, kolkhoznik*) is, in the present discussion, only a member of a collective farm. The category *employee* (*sluzhashchii*) includes office workers, low-, medium-, and high-grade employees who do not primarily do manual work, extending to those with managerial status.

well-being, including, to mention but three, those on education, health, and migration control. Other types of state activity, such as relations with foreign countries, both political and economic, may also have their subtle, or not so subtle, effects on social well-being. In addition, despite Gorbachev's evident dominance of the topmost political organs, political interplay among leading figures cannot be excluded as possible influences on the matters under investigation. These are all very broad questions, however, and though undoubtedly of interest, must be excluded from our study.

The Prospects for Living Standards

The social and economic development of the Soviet Union is conventionally held to be a matter of national planning, as registered in the directives of the five-year plans. Our first task, therefore, will be to see what the current, twelfth such plan has promised the public as a whole, and the less privileged people in particular, by the end of 1990. Well-being depends, however, not only on plan figures but also on plan fulfillment, and past experience demonstrates that this is by no means certain. After rises, albeit erratic ones, in the late 1950s and 1960s, the rate of economic growth tended to lag badly behind published promise. Gorbachev only confirmed what Western analysts had long believed when he stated that between the early 1970s and the mid-1980s, the rate of growth of national income had dropped by more than half, and that most planned goals had not been achieved. He also admitted that registered economic growth over the last four plan periods had depended largely on alcohol sales and oil revenues. Any discussion of prospects for raising living standards must take this sad experience into account.[3]

The Twelfth Plan was approved by the Supreme Soviet in June 1986, after, it would appear, a number of difficult revisions. As published, the final version was, as usual, brief and somewhat vague, but when supplemented with specialist comment served as a fairly good indicator of government intentions. The provisions of the plan most relevant to living standards may be summarized under three broad headings: income, food and consumer-good supplies, and housing. Let us consider each of these in turn.

Wages and Income

The plan promises an overall growth of 14.7 percent in the wages of workers and employees by 1990. This growth implies that the nominal monthly average would rise from 195.6 rubles to about 218 rubles over the five-year period. I use the word *nominal* since current deductions for income tax, holiday contributions, and trade-union dues would reduce the 1990 pay packet to about 174 rubles, which is close to the nominal figure given in the statistical handbooks for 1981.[4] Collective farmers, on the other hand, are supposed to do rather better, in that their average income from the public sector is supposed to rise by 18 percent (from around 153 rubles to 181 rubles). In 1985 they still obtained a quarter of their total income from their household, or "private," plots; however, a factor that must be taken into account in assessing their income is the extra labor that the plots demand. In addition, the plan contains promises of marginal income-tax concessions for the lower-paid.

Overall, what the Soviet statisticians call "real per capita income" is supposed to rise by 14 percent, and payments from the "social consumption funds" (used for financing education, health care, and pensions, and so on) are supposed to go up by a quarter. The actual meaning of the figures is something non-Soviet investigators are constantly seeking to ascertain, but even as they stand, the promises are modest indeed, when one takes into account the low living standards, the likely depredations of inflation (on which I shall comment below), and, of course, the period of time involved.

There is also the question of whether the promises are, in this case, likely to be kept. Looking back, we see that the Eleventh Five-Year Plan (1981– 1985) forecast a growth of 14.5 percent in wages for workers and employees, and 20 percent for peasants. Yet when inflation is left aside, the declared rises for these two groups were 12.6 percent and 29.7 percent, respectively. As for real per capita income, 16.5 percent was promised, and 10.9 percent apparently achieved. Over the same period, however, even the official indexes register price increases of about 5 percent; and, given the nature of Soviet marketing, actual rises were probably higher. Foreign estimates of the "real" increase in per capita consumption, made using the official figures, were of a little more than 1 percent per year. This was a most disappointing performance and must cast a dark shadow on the future.

The Twelfth Plan also lists certain specific categories of toilers whose earnings were to be raised, presumably because they were thought not to be receiving their just rewards. These groups included teachers and other educational workers and staff in the health services, cultural institutions, higher education, and research—what we might term the underprivileged intelligentsia. The actual increases were, however, unspecified. Workers in inhospitable geographical areas formerly not covered by regional bonus schemes were promised inclusion in these benefits, and workers on second and third shifts were to get extra incentives in comparison with those on first shifts.

Food and Consumer Goods

The availability of food in the USSR depends primarily on the performance of the agricultural sector. Soviet agriculture, however, suffers from a generally unfavorable climate and has traditionally been neglected by the powers that be. Improvements of a few percentage points in output, even over a number of years, have turned out to be no guarantee against further falls. Imports of grain and other products, though at times significant in absolute terms, have always been regarded as marginal to home produce and no answer to the basic problems of shortage.

With regard to food, the Twelfth Five-Year Plan allows for an overall (*valovoi*) increase of 14.4 percent by 1990, to be attained partly through a 21.4 percent rise in labor productivity in the public sector and, it would seem, by further encouragement of the private sector. In 1984 agricultural output was said to be 11 percent above that of 1980. This again was disappointing, but it lay behind Gorbachev's claim that the new plan figure in fact represented a doubling of the rate of growth of output. It must be remembered, of course, when making comparisons with past years, or indeed thinking of the future, that any absolute increases of output must be viewed against population growth, which generates more consumers. Judging by natural increase in 1986, a total population over 4 percent greater than at present, that is, numbering around 290 million people, is likely by 1990. Apart from this, achievement of the plan figures is again doubtful, and continuing food shortages are seemingly inevitable. It has also been suggested that increasingly unfavorable terms of trade may hinder supplementation from abroad of what is produced within the Soviet Union.

As for consumer goods, the plan envisages that supplies will grow faster than personal incomes. The increase in the output of branch "B" of industry, which produces most such goods, has been set at 27 percent, in contrast with 24.3 percent for branch "A," consisting of heavy industry. This also signals an intention to improve the balance of production in favor of the consumer. Yet the results of the Eleventh Plan are not encouraging. Branch "B" was then supposed to grow by 26.2 percent, but attained an increase of only 21 percent. The output of light industry, which produces clothing and footwear, is now to increase by 21 percent, but reached a growth of only 8 percent over the preceding five years. Retail trade has been assigned one of the largest increases: 33.4 percent. This goal must, though, be compared with the 23-percent growth of the previous plan, and the declared improvement of 16 percent.[5] Quality and delivery of consumer goods continue to be unsatisfactory. The indexes for the consumer sector may be subject to some slight upward revision as the private sector expands, and one awaits with interest the statistical reporting that greater private enterprise may engender.

Housing Stocks

The shortage of housing is another widely recognized problem, for under Soviet rule many, perhaps a majority, of citizens have been obliged to spend their lives in slum conditions. The figure for new building (defined as "general usable space in dwelling houses") given in the current plan is no less than 559 million square meters; but judging from the past record, the prospects for attainment of the set goal are good. The Eleventh Five-Year Plan envisaged the construction of 530 million square meters, and some 552.2 million apparently came into existence. Of all consumer needs, this seems to be the one regarding which the government has enjoyed its steadiest successes.

Nevertheless, the figures for new building are rather less impressive when translated into habitable living space, and viewed in the context of the total living space available in the USSR. For then account has to be taken of space lost through demolition, delapidation, and poor quality (especially in the countryside), as well as of misleading statistical practice. Between 1980 and 1985, for example, the overall increase in the fund of existing space came to about 1.8 square meters per dweller. But in terms of actual living area (excluding corridors, kitchens, bathrooms, and other ancillary floorage) it was only about 1.1 square meters. This in turn took the national per capita average up to about nine square meters, which was still very cramped by West European standards. Sharing is still widespread: in 1984 up to a fifth of the urban population was so registered, usually, one presumes, in the traditional "communal" flats.[6]

The Twelfth Five-Year Plan would seem to promise, when all these factors, together with population growth, are taken into account, a little more than another square meter per capita. Seemingly, an acute problem will remain. The best that can be said is that people in the most unsatisfactory housing conditions, and those who have been waiting longest, usually enjoy some priority in re-housing. By and large, local authorities endeavor to allot accommodation to those who need it most.

The General Outlook

Given these patterns, what are the prospects for raising living standards overall? With regard to fulfillment of the plan as a whole, national utilized income is supposed to increase by 22.1 percent by 1990, which implies an annual growth of over 4 percent throughout the period. In Soviet terms this is ambitious, as it means just about doubling the rate of growth of the last plan period. In the first two years of the current plan, growth of 4.1 and

2.3 percent, respectively, was achieved. Moreover, most of the indexes we have mentioned here: workers' and peasants' wages, real income, the output of branch "B" of industry, and important types of agricultural production, failed to meet the targeted growth rates.

The promised improvements depend heavily on increases in labor productivity, which is expected to rise by as much as 25 percent in industry. But in this respect, too, both industry and agriculture have so far failed to achieve planned increases. Improving productivity lies, of course, at the core of Gorbachev's master design for economic reorganization. Factors hindering such improvement, apart from the frictions of reorganization itself, include stricter verification of goods produced (*gospriemka*) with consequent higher rejection rates, the inbuilt inflexibility of the administration, and, in the longer term, progressive exhaustion of the more accessible raw materials. Sociologists might add that a discontented work force could also act as a powerful retardant.[7]

Not surprisingly, many outside observers have become pessimistic about the chances of success for the Twelfth Five-Year Plan, and some have already declared it a failure. In a careful summary of the development of personal income up to the spring of 1988, for example, Gertrude Schroeder suggested that per capita consumption, according to the most revealing Soviet data, registered a growth of between 1 and 2 percent over the three years 1985–1987, but "use of a Western-style price index and measures of real per capita consumption would show an overall decline in living standards over this period."[8] Part of the problem, she contended, lay in the ineptness of the anti-alcohol campaign launched under Iurii Andropov. This indeed resulted in a massive fall in legal sales, but it also cut treasury receipts, left more money in people's pockets, contributed vastly to inflationary pressures, and led to widespread bootlegging. Gorbachev's own utterances, particularly his speech at the February 1988 plenum of the Central Committee, suggested increasing desperation with the overall state of affairs.

The picture becomes even more somber when one considers how modest the promises of the Twelfth Five-Year Plan are by West European standards. The purchasing power of the ruble is low, and inflation is significant. The years pass with little perceptible change in the street or in the workplace. Furthermore, any registered improvement in Soviet living standards must be judged not only against the levels currently enjoyed in capitalist lands, but also against the advances that capitalist economies may expect to achieve in the future. Many have been doing reasonably well in recent years: between 1976 and 1985 increases of between 20 and 30 percent in personal consumption rates were not unusual. Over the three years 1983–1986, Great Britain chalked up an advance of about 10 percent in personal disposable income. So even successful attainment of the main plan targets would leave a massive gap between the Soviet and many capitalist consumers.[9]

Thus most of the information available on the Twelfth Five-Year Plan suggests that it is too ambitious and therefore infeasible. Indeed, some observers think it entirely unrealistic to organize a far-reaching reform of the economy and of the labor force and to plan substantial production increases at the same time. It may be that as a consequence the pressures on the Gorbachev leadership will become intolerable. If the plan is indeed not fulfilled, past experience suggests that the consumer, rather than the administration, the military, or the investment sector, will suffer. But if the leadership can demonstrate some success in its endeavors and manage to instill more positive public attitudes toward productive labor, the outlook will perhaps be less gloomy.

The Drive Against Equal Incomes

The problem of distributing rewards in society is hardly less important than ensuring plenty. One of the most notable features of Gorbachev's thinking is his dislike of the kind of egalitarianism that had been taken for granted in the USSR for some three decades. Indeed, some of his antiegalitarian utterances, including the specific attacks on wage leveling, had a curious resemblance to Stalin's. Since his advent to supreme power, he has made no secret of his belief that "harmful leveling" has contributed vastly to the slowdown in Soviet economic advance. His response has been to replace it with a more vigorous social philosophy, albeit within the framework of Marxism-Leninism.

The background to this problem is not without interest. Soviet leaderships, though always cognizant of the need for some social differentiation and protective of the privileges of the topmost elite, have pursued quite different aims with regard to egalitarianism. There is no doubt that Lenin favored a relatively even distribution of rewards, but, as we have shown elsewhere, he soon had to make concessions to key groups of supporters. Stalin, in a famous speech to industrial managers in 1931, actually criticized egalitarian income policies, which came to be described as "harmful." For the remainder of his rule he promoted a type of social differentiation that was supposed to reflect loyalty to the regime and labor input.[10]

Khrushchev's de-Stalinization campaign brought far-reaching change. The privileges of the political elite were somewhat curtailed, while at the lower end of the social spectrum a minimum wage was reintroduced, social security improved, and help given to the peasantry. Khrushchev also instituted a reform of the wage system designed to narrow what he considered to be the excessive differentials that his predecessor had encouraged. Brezhnev took less interest in such mundane matters, but allowed differentials to narrow further, while again bolstering some of the older elitist privileges.

Problems of Pay Differentiation

Given Gorbachev's beliefs about the harmfulness of these developments, a major reform of the wage and salary system was virtually inevitable. This was, however, no easy matter, for the system had long since assumed a monstrous and ironclad character. In the West wages tend to be determined by market forces, to the extent that employees bargain with employers, individually or through trade unions. Even when rates of pay are set by a government body, they usually reflect market pressures. In the Soviet Union, on the other hand, genuine bargaining is almost unknown. The wage system is controlled by a massive body of state law and regulation, covering basic pay, bonuses, and pay differentials for state employees in all branches of the economy. It has always been plagued by distortions that overencourage or hinder individual effort, depending on their nature. Regardless of its policy towards egalitarianism, almost every Soviet leadership has felt compelled to try to effect some improvement in the wage system.

Gorbachev's own reform was embodied in the decree of 17 September 1986. It provided for a new, more differentiated system of remuneration throughout the productive sector of the economy, which employed nearly three quarters of the nonpeasant work force. The complexity of the measure may be judged from the official commentary on it, which ran to 40 closely printed pages. For present purposes, however, six main features may be distinguished.[11]

The first was a new concept of the wage fund, based not on mere plan fulfillment, but on good-quality output, sales achieved, and savings made from reorganization and staff reduction. Clearly, this implied differentiation insofar as efficient enterprises would end up paying their workers more than inefficient ones. Second, wage rates were supposed to rise significantly. Over the period of the Twelfth Five-Year Plan, as we have noted, the majority of workers should expect a 20–25 percent increase in their tariffs, while the relatively small number employed in technically advanced production jobs could look forward to increases of 45–50 percent. These increases, however, were to be based on enterprise performance, improved productivity, and upward reassessments of labor norms. They were problematic for many.

Third, the long-term trend towards equalization of basic wage rates, regardless of skill, effort, and responsibility, was to be reversed. When left to function of its own accord, the wage system had tended to allow wages to "creep" upward at the bottom of the range of skill gradings, while hindering increases at the top. Rising state-set minimal wages exacerbated this tendency. As a result, the ratio between rates of pay for bottom and top skill gradings had narrowed to 1:1.5 or 1:1.6, which was unfair to the people at the top. As a consequence of the reform, new scales were proposed to widen it to 1:1.8, and in some branches of industry, to more than that. This change, however, would also affect the bonuses paid, so differentials between take-home pay packets would be greater. In fact, by the early 1980s the ratio between the bottom and top 10 percent of take-home earnings was said to be about 1:3.0.[12]

Fourth, the system of bonuses was itself to be changed, to effect tighter control of payments and make them more dependent on contributions to output. According to the veteran labor economist L. A. Kostin (*Pravda*, 17 February 1987), the basic wage, which was supposed to be the principal component of the pay packet, was nationally down to 50 percent of total pay. This meant that the remainder was made up of ill-controlled bonuses and supplements that did not necessarily reflect work done.

Next, the decree envisaged an increase in the general pay differential between workers (or less-skilled personnel) and qualified specialists. Kostin revealed that the average gap had shrunk to a mere 10 percent, as against 46 percent in the mid-1960s. In fact, in the construction and machine-building industries specialists were receiving less than ordinary workers. It is not, of course, unknown for Soviet degree holders to take manual jobs to increase their income. Specialists' salaries were now expected to rise by 30–45 percent, depending on the importance and technological state of their organization or enterprise.

Finally, the wage reform was to be integrated with other important economic measures, which included giving the enterprise more independence, granting it the authority to make certain agreements of a commercial character, and extending managerial power. Brigade or group working practices, especially on a contractual basis, were to be extended throughout the labor force. The introduction of such contracts was also intended to be differentiative, both among and inside brigades, insofar as earnings were to be distributed strictly according to labor input, or, as it was now quaintly termed, the "coefficient of labor participation."

The whole wage reform was aimed at encouraging honest effort and matching it with due reward. It was not, therefore, crudely elitist in orientation. Many people in protected managerial positions undoubtedly stood to lose from both the new emphasis on efficiency and the proposed changes in selection procedures, were they to be implemented (a matter we return to later in this chapter). The reform was soon backed by a press campaign against "unhealthy leveling," unearned income, and what Gorbachev considered to be unfair privileges. Access to the foreign-currency stores for Soviet employees with foreign connections was reported to have been stopped in January 1988, while the awarding of state honors to the undeserving was publicly criticized in April.[13]

If Gorbachev's emphasis on payment according to results is not necessarily elitist, it is not—to digress for a moment—obviously Marxist, either. According to the oft-quoted formula, the first stage of communism is characterized by payment according to labor, which surely means personal input, and the second stage by payment according to need. The idea of rewarding toilers according to *result* takes the matter into another dimension.

The wage-reform law was followed by the usual body of supportive legislation, including appropriate clauses in Gorbachev's new law on state enterprises published in *Izvestiia* on 1 July 1987. These clauses placed considerable emphasis on "the use of pay as the most important way of stimulating the growth of productivity, accelerating scientific progress, and improving the quality and effectiveness of production" (Article 14, Section 5). The enterprise would be able to determine its own pay systems, "not allowing for wage leveling." It could set up workplaces with higher rates of pay, extend "second job" practices, and give extra pay to people working unsociable hours (that is, on second and third shifts). It could also set salaries for managers and specialists without reference to their numbers or to the average salary within the enterprise, which had been well-known constraints in the past. It could also fix the usage of incentive funds, and set its own bonuses for managers, construction experts, and technologists.

The proof of this hefty pudding will again be in the eating, but present indications suggest that digestion of it will be slow. Wage reform, as part of enterprise reorganization, had been expected to proceed in industry, agriculture, construction, transport, and communication at a fairly brisk pace: 15 percent completion by 1987; 55 percent by 1988; and 100 percent by 1990. It appears that by September 1987 only about 4.5 percent of the staff in these branches had been switched over to the new system. Such figures, backed by Gorbachev's unending complaints about obstruction, suggest that the implementation of wage reform will still be far from complete by the end of the decade.[14]

In any case the kind of differentiation now envisaged, whether more or less great than that promoted by Stalin, must benefit primarily well-qualified, energetic workers, younger specialists with good career prospects, and those employed in efficient enterprises. People in poorly paid, less skilled jobs and those in less successful enterprises are likely to find themselves at the bottom of a higher pyramid. They will gain only as average living standards rise throughout Soviet society. It is perhaps noteworthy that no less a figure than Sergei Kretov, head of the wages section of the USSR State Committee for

Labor and Social Questions, wrote approvingly of the possible need to introduce a "colossal" wage differential of a factor "even of ten, such as the Stakhanovites earned in their day."[15]

This may be why the social implications of the reform, subtle or crude, found so little mention in the copious comments that followed it. For instance, the prominent sociologist L. A. Gordon, reviewing the history of social policy and wage differentials up to 1987, might have been expected to consider the development of new socio-occupational groups, or the strains and stresses likely to be engendered. Instead he dwelled on the deleterious effects of wage egalitarianism. In the long run, he claimed, equal wages tended to promote unhealthy ideas and damage people's attitudes to their work; respect for a hard-earned wage disappeared. People developed instead either an indiscriminate admiration for high earnings, regardless of their source, or an envy of anyone significantly better off than themselves.[16]

The spirit of the wage reform may also explain why Gorbachev has never expressed any particular public interest in the minimum wage. In the past it had been a prominent propaganda tool. A source of genuine pride to the early Bolshevik leadership, it dropped out of sight in the 1930s, but was reestablished, as we have noted, by Khrushchev. Set at the equivalent of 27–35 rubles, according to the branch of the economy, in 1956, it was gradually raised until it reached 70 rubles in the Brezhnev years. A new nationwide minimum of 80 rubles was promised as part and parcel of the Eleventh Five-Year Plan, but the promise was abandoned and, as a note in the 1985 statistical handbook attests, only workers in the mining industry benefited from it.

The 80-ruble figure has now been carried forward, it is said, for implementation in the current plan period. Obviously, Gorbachev must have been privy to discussion of this matter but wishes to leave the government with as much freedom of *manoeuvre* as possible. Beyond the emphasis on more differentiated payment by results, the lower-paid workers are thus given to understand that they cannot expect an ever-rising floor under their feet. Their interests, as a group, are to be overridden by the exigencies of economic efficiency.

New Taxation and Pricing Policies?

Until recently, Soviet wage policy could be thought of as complete in itself, inasmuch as both income tax and inflation tended to be low and relatively stable. Change has been evident here, too, however, and wage policy can no longer be considered without reference to them. Let us deal with the tax situation first.

Soviet tax history has seen some curious twists and turns, but the present rates, set out in the decree of 20 October 1983, departed little from principles established as long ago as April 1943. Direct taxation is not used as an instrument for massive redistribution or punitive extraction, as in capitalist lands, and the ceiling for workers and employees has remained at an enviably low 13 percent. The main changes between 1943 and 1983 consisted mainly in reductions in tax liability for the low-paid and the unmarried and for poorer families, accompanied by increases in liability for other workers as their wages rose. According to the national average family budget figures, income tax and associated payments made by the average worker and employee rose only from 7.3 percent of total income (including government subsidies) in 1970 to 8.3 percent in 1985.[17]

Gorbachev mentioned the need for reform in this domain, too, and some public discussion took place. In an authoritative article written in October 1986, the wage economists S. Shatalin and V. Grebnikov indicated a possible course of action. It was not easy for them to explain away practices, and indeed principles, that had been observed for decades; thus their utterances were rather opaque. The task of income tax, they wrote, was "to regulate socioeconomic relations . . . and bring them into line with the current conditions of national development." Although, in the end, rising prosperity would obviate the need for redistribution, income tax was still required as "an additional means of regulating workers' and employees' incomes," especially in view of the proposed changes in the economic mechanism.[18]

More specifically, the writers suggested increasing taxes on private enterprise in cases where the latter appeared to be getting out of hand, and, more surprisingly, establishing a flexible, but "sharply progressive scale" for wages and salaries in general. This would ease the pressure of indirect taxation (primarily by means of purchase taxes) and could be used to remove extra earnings received through windfalls or cyclical factors. It would do away with the need for frequent revisions of the tax code and could mop up excessive or even illegal income.

Apparently, if Shatalin's and Grebnikov's proposals were followed, taxation would be made more direct and healthier, while a brake would be put into place that would be applied should the differentiation drive get out of hand. They did, however, show some awareness of social consequences and made encouraging reference to the fate of the lower-paid. Income tax, they thought, should be directed mainly at earnings in the upper part of the pay scale: "The very nature of the tax's function indicates that the minimum earnings not subject to taxation should be substantially higher than the current minimum and, in our view, close to the average wage."

A number of changes in income taxation were in fact approved in the course of 1987. They included exemption for young couples in their first year of married life (granted in January) and some reduction of the income taxes paid by collective farms (approved in June). A decree passed in April

introduced more flexible categorization of private enterprise and some reduction in the rates payable by them.[19] The basic scales, as confirmed in
1983, were left in place, however. The authorities apparently had rejected
(at least for the time being) any strongly progressive taxation of the majority
of toilers. This stance seems to accord with the current wage policy.

Given the relatively low standard of living in the USSR, retail prices are a
particularly sensitive matter. Astonishing though it may appear to anyone
unversed in Soviet reality, official policy has long been to control virtually all
prices in the state sector and hold them unchanged for years at a time. The
result—according to the economist Nikolai Shmelev, whose work we discuss below—is a massive list of 24 million authorized prices, which, as often
as not, fail to reflect supply or demand and thus exacerbate both shortages
and surpluses of goods. The state takes huge mark-ups—a concealed purchase tax—on consumer durables, while subsidizing foodstuffs, housing, and
other social amenities. Subsidies on basic products apparently amounted to
17 percent of the state budget in 1986 and had been rising steadily. As a
result of much decreased vodka sales and poor performance in agriculture
and the consumer-goods industries, inflationary pressures have tended to increase greatly. Between 1980 and 1986, for example, the volume of personal
savings, which may serve as a pointer of potential demand, grew by no less
than 64 percent and averaged the equivalent of seven months' wages per
account.[20]

Formal price control has allowed the government to claim that inflation is
minimal and that real wages are rising. Declared price increases have been
rare and narrow in application; price reductions, on the other hand, receive
considerable publicity. Low pricing of essentials, though questionable in
economic terms, has also been of undoubted benefit to the poorer parts of
society. But the realities of inflation nevertheless make themselves felt, and,
as may be seen from some of the material presented in chapter 4, the public
is intensely aware of them. Handy indicators, from the point of view of the
man in the street, include prices at the collective-farm markets (where levels
have been two and a half times more than those of state shops), change of
quality, rebranding of common state-produced goods, overt price rises for
capital purchases (like cars and flats), and, of course, the actual sums paid
for black-market goods and services.

Gorbachev has publicly stressed the need to reform this stultified system
and bring it closer to economic realities. Legislative proposals were supposed to be mooted by the bodies most involved in the fourth quarter of
1986. As of spring 1988, though, retail pricing (like the tax system) had un-
dergone no substantive change. In his speech to the 27th Party Congress,
Gorbachev also referred to the need to introduce more realistic and differentiated rents in the state sector. Obviously he was looking to move away

from the system of extremely low charges (usually a fraction of a ruble per square meter) that had been in effect since the late 1920s. The most obvious explanation for delay in these matters is the danger of highly unfavorable social responses at a time when the Soviet leadership is coping with opposition in many other spheres.[21]

At the same time commentators seem to take three things for granted. First, there is a real need for reform, and even for bringing the pattern of Soviet prices more into line with those of other advanced countries. Second, whatever happens, the state must retain a considerable degree of control; and third, any change must be cautious and protect the interests of the most vunerable members of Soviet society. Most Soviet families still spend a large portion of their income on food and other essentials, and any price increases would need to be preceded by fair warning and a reorientation of public attitudes.

It is hazardous to comment further at the present time, but a proposal made by G. Chubakov in January 1987 may give an indication of future trends, if only because it is very "Soviet" in spirit. Retail goods, he wrote, could be categorized into five groups and priced accordingly. The groups were (1) essential foods and consumer durables of particular social importance that required low and stable pricing, that is, heavy subsidization; (2) common cultural and consumer goods, which should be priced sympathetically but with regard to costs and social need; (3) other common consumer goods, which should be priced to reflect real aggregate production costs; (4) goods in short supply of a specific or prestigious character, such as delicatessen foods and stylish clothes, which should be retailed at their real economic cost; and (5) popular but harmful products, such as alcohol and tobacco, which should be priced at socially discouraging levels. It will be interesting to see how pricing develops if the Gorbachev leadership continues its present course.[22]

Private Enterprise Encouraged

Gorbachev's public references to the possibility of encouraging a modest degree of private enterprise evoked considerable interest both in the USSR and abroad, not least because they recalled, albeit superficially, Lenin's economic volte-face of 1921. The new policy was prompted by economic considerations, primarily the widespread deficits of goods and services, but it must also be regarded as part of the shift toward a more internally differentiated society. It was effectively launched with the promulgation, on 19 November 1986, of the Law on Individual Private Enterprise, together with a number of subsidiary regulations. These were followed, in June 1988, by a detailed law giving greater scope for private enterprise in the form of officially registered cooperatives with a minimum membership of three. The cooperatives were to enjoy considerable legal protection and were in some respects (social security, for example) equated with state enterprises. Work in them was declared to be prestigious and worthy of encouragement. Many cooperatives, however, were apparently established on the basis of the 1986 measure, and since the 1988 law has only just appeared, the comments that follow will be restricted largely to its predecessor.[23]

The 1986 law replaced the vaguer, and generally more restrictive, instructions of May 1976, which simply permitted activities involving "the production of items for sale to the public and the provision of paid household (*bytovye*) services." In practice, however, other activities, including small repairs and personal services, had also been lawful, especially outside large towns, and were listed as such in legal handbooks. Beyond that, the income-tax regulations specifically authorized earnings from private medical practice, teaching, architectural drawing, artistic effort, and typing. We must not forget in this connection the encouragement of private agriculture (especially since the late 1970s) and the practice of contracting out piecework by local enterprises.[24]

The 1986 measure was nevertheless a major concession in that it specified and underpinned at a national level a broad range of activities. These included the production of clothes, furniture, toys, and other artifacts; services such as hairdressing, typing and bookbinding, private transport, care of the disabled, and letting accommodation; private coaching in sewing and music and in shorthand and typing; translation and medical practice; and the production of decorative and traditional articles. The measure contained 29 items in all, with additional clauses for unspecified activities "not forbidden by law." Gone was an older regulation prohibiting the issue of licenses for two or more unrelated individuals to work together in the same room.

Of all the policies we have considered so far, this one was probably discussed most candidly in the Soviet media, especially insofar as it pertained to satisfying unfulfilled consumer demand. The economists B. Bolotskii and S. Golovnin, writing in July 1987, stated that although according to certain estimates Soviet citizens annually spent 40 billion hours shopping (a figure yielding a weekly total of about four hours per adult), in half of the cases they failed to find what they sought. Larger pay packets, the economists continued, were not matched by increased supplies of goods, and the inflated savings that they generated could be valued at nearly a third of personal possessions. Meanwhile, the USSR Ministry of Trade was losing about four billion rubles on unusable goods annually, while unsatisfied demand for services was costed at five to six billion rubles. In fact, the evidence presented in the next chapter indicates that the problems of deficit were even more widespread and serious.[25]

As for the extent of individual private enterprise before 1986, I. I. Gladkii, chairman of the USSR State Committee for Labor and Social Questions, calmly put the figure at a modest 100,000 participants. This, however, grotesquely underrepresented the situation and may have covered only officially registered practitioners. There is no lack of evidence that unregistered activity—the so-called second economy—was extensive. A recent sociological study in West Siberia indicated that no less than 17 percent of the work force spent some of their free time earning money, which was mostly undeclared for tax purposes. Even this may have been an underestimate, for our own survey of emigré families (presented below) showed that nearly half of the adults questioned had engaged in undeclared private enterprise, either in their working or free time, and that across the whole sample some 12 percent of family income was derived from it.

A striking indication of mass evasion was provided by the Moscow City Finance Department itself. It reported that only three people had registered themselves as private typists in the whole of the metropolis, others (probably hundreds) having failed to do so in order to avoid paying tax. For the sphere of domestic services as a whole, Bolotskii and Golovnin quoted a string of impressive figures for private provision thereof: of shoe repairs—50 percent; of household decoration—43 percent; technical household repairs—30 percent; car repairs—65 percent; general services in rural areas—up to 80 percent. Even house construction figured in their list at 8 percent. In all, a labor force of 1.7–2.0 million persons was thought to be involved in private services and activities. These figures evidently did not include moonlighting (illegal or impermissible work) at the workplace.[26]

The possibilities offered by the 1986 law should not be overestimated. Although the provisions of the 1988 measure on cooperatives are more promising, there can be no question of private enterprise being allowed to endanger the massive predominance of state production and services. The traditional ideological barriers against an economically important private sector remain firmly in place. The primary aim of the 1986 measure, at least, was to encourage legal enterprise among the retired or underemployed, without diverting able-bodied individuals from work in the state sector. Significantly, individual private enterprise did not count as employment for pension purposes, and full-time engagement in it lasting more than three months disrupted the pensionable service record. Potential loss of income in old age must have been a disincentive for many.

At an administrative level the local soviets have been granted wide, and apparently increasing, powers of supervision and suppression. Inevitably, reports of obstruction have abounded. Individual enterprise has to be licensed, normally for a year at a time in any given locality. Furthermore, the 1986 law contained prohibitions that apparently exceeded the normal requirements of public well-being. They banned work with animal skins, precious metals or stones, games of chance or baths, certain medical practices, study not included in regular state curricula, and theatrical entertainment. Gainful activities could be halted if they were held to contradict public interest, though not if they merely competed with state enterprises. The new law did, however, contain a provision for appealing decisions prohibiting particular instances of private enterprise.

Furthermore, activities that were actually found to be illegal were classed together with such nefarious deeds as embezzlement, bribery, and speculation and subjected to more severe sanctions. Gorbachev himself spoke out against abuses that "contradicted the economic norms and moral ideals of Soviet society" (*Pravda*, 24 April 1985). An important edict of the Presidium of the Supreme Soviet of 23 May 1986 increased existing fines and terms of imprisonment. In addition, private transactions involving sums of 10,000 rubles or more (20,000 in the case of house construction) had to be declared to local authorities, and the source of the funds revealed. The press campaign that followed was intended to serve as a warning to offenders, but may also have reflected the attitudes of a conservative lobby.[27]

These impediments probably explain the relative slowness of the response to Gorbachev's initiative. By July 1987 only about 137,000 Soviet citizens— about one per thousand of the national labor force—had gained permission to start businesses. Also, the number of applications was only a third or a quarter of what had been expected. By January 1988 the number of new cooperatives had reached 8,000, and although this might seem impressive at first sight, they still employed less than 0.4 percent of the labor force and competed with the 303,000 state enterprises already providing services of a domestic type. Some cooperatives failed at an early stage, while others were criticized for paying their organizers excessive wages. Generalizations about the difficulties faced in this sector were common.[28]

With regard to the social impact of private enterprise, much remains unclear. Since many different kinds of activity will be undertaken, the consequences must vary. Many who are now moonlighting may be persuaded to register. Beyond this there must be some encouragement for newcomers and the establishment of long-lasting personal businesses, particularly if living standards and demand rise. Activities such as catering and the use of private vehicles as taxi cabs seem to be reported most frequently. Obviously, economic incentives will be paramount. A private catering business in Moscow, for example, was recently yielding earnings of 500–600 rubles a month. It is almost self-evident that pay packets in the private sector must be significantly higher than in the state sector to attract participation. Beyond that, however, some people may enjoy the excitement of having their own business or working outside a state organization.

No proper analysis of the social background of the "privateers" has so far come to our notice. A short account of such activity in the Saratov oblast, however, revealed that over 60 percent of them were pensioners who saw such work as a way of increasing their income. Existing pensions were not affected. Nearly all other participants were already in full-time employment; thus only a small residue of the people who opted exclusively for the private sector were in employable age groups.[29] In the country as a whole, pensioners who choose to extend their working lives may indeed gain financially, as may persons who can somehow utilize to their advantage the patterns of deficit of goods and services. But real commercial success must hinge greatly on possessing modest capital, the connections needed to procure raw material, and money for bribery. It is likely that the principal benefits will go to people already well up in the socioeconomic hierarchy. Private enterprise, like church membership, will probably be shunned by those anxious to enjoy the traditional benefits of a party-based career.

There is no reason, of course, why small-scale private enterprise should not, as in some of the people's democracies, coexist indefinitely with widespread deprivation. The kind of capitalism most likely to emerge from the stony soil of Soviet socialism will presumably resemble what Max Weber termed "speculative" capitalism—an unhealthy variety, the built-in limitations and uncertain future of which encourage illegality and make it the object of social disdain.

We should, perhaps, conclude our survey of Gorbachev's antiegalitarian policies by sounding a further unsettling note. Not only are these policies innovative, provocative, and of uncertain future; they are also, apparently, being supplemented by others no less differentiative in the spheres of education and medicine. Thus a resolution of the plenum of the Central Committee passed in February 1988 expressed profound dissatisfaction with Soviet education as it had developed in recent years. The resolution proposed, in addition to more vocational training, some differentiation in the courses offered by general schools, and contractual links between advanced educational institutions and the enterprises for which they train specialists. That is, enterprises receiving graduates from such institutions would be expected to take more financial responsibility for their training. Elements of these policies can, of course, be traced back to the 1960s and earlier; but present indications are that the structure of education will become less unitary.

In the sphere of health care Gorbachev has set the task of improving standards, which most foreign observers consider to be appalling and partly responsible for the country's poor health picture. A new general law, published in *Pravda* on 27 November 1987, prescribed upgrading the status of the medical profession and differentiating the pay of its members; introducing commercial relations between medical institutions and the enterprises they serve, obliging the latter to pay for medical services rendered to their staff; giving patients access to better-grade hospitalization at their own expense and the possibility of buying better-quality meals when in hospital; and in general encouraging private endeavor in health care. It will be interesting to observe the social effects of these measures, if and when they are implemented; but the intention to move away from egalitarian provision of health services is clear.

Job Security—Some Dangers Appear

The provision of employment must loom large in any enlightened social program, regardless of the nature of the economy on which it is based. It is not surprising, then, that Gorbachev's speeches have included many references to labor problems, and in particular that of manpower surpluses. He appears to believe that the oft-proclaimed "shortages" of labor in the Soviet Union are more apparent than real and due in no small measure to the retention of uneconomic equipment and outdated work practices. In the same vein, commentators have recently expressed growing concern about the large number of jobs in less efficient sectors of the economy and the need to redeploy workers elsewhere. Although Gorbachev has publicly denied any intention to tolerate unemployment in the USSR, the industrial regeneration that he is promoting has certainly raised new and specific threats to job security.

Until recently, such security had been regarded as almost sacrosanct. The Soviet worker had been told for decades that though earnings in the USSR might be lower than in capitalist lands, the horrible specter of unemployment was absent. Its presence was denied after Stalin had banished the term from official discourse, and eliminated any benefits that went with the condition, in October 1930. Subsequent plan-fulfillment reports proudly proclaimed that unemployment did not exist. Various types of "idleness" may have been sporadically admitted in the press—among school-leavers, workers changing jobs, residents of small towns, and members of Islamic communities, for example. It was claimed that such instances were transient or statistically insignificant, however.

The terms of the labor contract signed by most Soviet workers and employees did, indeed, make casual dismissal difficult. The standard listing of circumstances under which it could take place included closure of the enterprise or general reductions of staff, the revealed unsuitability of the employee for his post, systematic violations of labor discipline, deliberate absence or long-term illness, and the return of a person who had occupied the same post previously. No proper statistics are available, but straightforward closures and extensive redundancies have probably been rare. The easiest way a management could rid itself of an unwanted employee was to find him or her unsuitable for the post in question. This, however, had to be proved, and the procedure could only be applied in individual cases. Also, the appeal system seems to have been quite effective and ensured a large proportion of reinstatements.[30]

Of course, a large and relatively inefficient economy, such as that of the USSR, must contain, in absolute terms, a fair number of people who cannot find satisfactory work, at least in the short term. Much more important is the problem of people who have jobs but are in fact underemployed, as their knowledge and capabilities are superfluous to real needs. It is this category that is of primary concern to the current leadership. Indications of changed official thinking are to be found in a number of new decrees on labor organization and in articles in newspapers and journals. Here we shall deal with the relevant legislation, leaving the media comment to the last chapter.

Enterprise Closure and Reorganization

The July 1987 law on state enterprises was meant to revitalize state-owned plants by increasing economic accountability, reducing planning constraints, and giving managers more freedom internally. It replaced a string of enactments going back to the nationalization decrees of the revolution and also a conservative, Brezhnev-style law of 1974. With regard to the weighty matters of plant closure or contraction, the latter had stated merely that power of decision lay with the body to which the enterprise belonged. The 1987 law, by contrast, dealt with closure in a specific and virtually unprecedented manner.[31]

It could take place "if the need for continuing work was removed, and [the enterprise] could not be reorganized, or on other grounds provided for by law"; "if the enterprise was loss-making, and providing no return over a long period"; "if there was no demand for its products"; and when "remedial measures for ensuring economic operation on the basis of self-financing" did not produce the desired results. The grounds for reorganization as such were not spelled out, but the decision to undertake it remained within the competence of the directorate to which the enterprise belonged (Article 23). In addition, the 1987 law gave managements more flexibility in fixing the size and qualifications of their labor forces, and in reducing the sums of money spent on "keeping administrative personnel" (Articles 2 and 14).

On the other hand, the text contained little by way of reassurance for dismissed workers. They were, it stated, to be guaranteed their constitutional rights (that is, the right to work), which is about as vague a formulation as could be used. They were to be "personally" informed of dismissal at least two months in advance, retain their average wage, and any uninterrupted service record "but not for more than three months." This meant that if they did not take other employment in this interval their pension rights could be reduced and that they could have problems with residence permits. The official bodies conducting the reorganization or closure, together with the local soviet, were to offer them "every assistance" in finding a job, but this fell short of a guarantee of desirable work. Claims or complaints against the newly liquidated enterprise could be made to "higher bodies." Workers who could not be placed in accordance with their training and skills should undertake to retrain, as set down in a new labor contract.

The Attestation of Workplaces

A related threat lay in the proposed "attestation" of workplaces, which became law in August 1985. The Soviet authorities had, for their own administrative reasons, long conducted periodic censuses of the national occupation structure. In the academic sphere, for instance, the "attestation" of the work and political qualities of employees (nota bene, of the persons rather than the jobs) had been common for at least three decades, and it was extended to schoolteachers, though with little effect, in the early 1970s. Given the interest of the Gorbachev leadership in labor efficiency, it was natural that some kind of inspection should be extended throughout the economy. The August decree, noting the successful attestation of workplaces in two vehicle-building industries and in certain oblasts, stipulated that the practice should now be extended to almost all production and trade organizations, including agriculture, by the end of 1987 and conducted annually thereafter.[32]

A network of attestation commissions was soon established with the participation of ministries, administrations, and local soviets throughout the country. The practical assessments, however, were left to local managers, with the formal assistance of the trade-union committees. No secret was made of the fact that the measure was intended to reduce surplus jobs and improve efficiency at all levels. Managers had to ensure the "revelation of workplaces that did not accord with progressive technical and organizational decisions, labor-protection rules, or the best work practices, norms and standards," and to ensure that they were "rationalized." Manual and heavy physical labor was, when possible, to be mechanized, workplaces with bad conditions and ineffective jobs eliminated, and better use made of existing equipment.[33]

Payment by Results

The proposed reorganization of the wage system was another threat to employment. An official commentary published soon after stated that the decree indeed presupposed the release of part of the employed work force. Ideally, an enlarged wage fund would be shared by fewer, better-employed people.[34]

The commentary also contained advice on the order of dismissal when a manager had some choice in the matter. Priority, it said, should be given to the most qualified and efficient workers and employees, identified as such through comments on their performance and training and examination of documents in their personal files. After these criteria had been applied, preference should be given to people in certain underprivileged categories: those with two or more dependents; single earners with dependents; persons with the longest service record at the enterprise; invalids; part-time students; persons whose parents had died during military service or were approaching retirement age; and single mothers. We cannot be sure that any proper sociological study of such dismissals will be published in the near future, but these proposals make it clear that the less efficient and less skilled workers, that is, the poorest, will be most vulnerable.

The commentary gave more advice on redeployment, retraining, and interim pay. When a worker is redeployed, for which his agreement is required, he is eligible for a month's pay, plus travel and family allowances while the move to the new post is taking place. He may also be paid during a three-month retraining period, all at the expense of the new enterprise. If, however, no work is available with or through his former employer, or if he does not accept what is offered, he is sent to one of the employment bureaus run by local soviets. These shall be discussed below.

It will be noted that the Gorbachev wage-reform documents contain no specific reference to unemployment pay. The silence is not fortuitous. This is still one of the most striking gaps in the Soviet social-security system, and Gorbachev has studiously avoided any commitment to fill it, apart from the rather modest redundancy payments already mentioned. Given the general drift of his policies, this, again, is not surprising.

Discipline and Conditions of Labor

Disciplinary pressures on the Soviet work force have had a tense history, going back to Trotskii's revolutionary labor armies and Stalin's militarization of the labor market. Gorbachev has repeatedly emphasized the need for strengthening labor discipline, reducing the number of absences, and suppressing alcohol consumption at the workplace. The present series of campaigns was started by Iurii Andropov in November 1982 as a response to the avowedly disastrous situation that had developed under Brezhnev. By the mid-1980s the USSR had one of the highest alcoholism rates in the world, and individual expenditures on alcohol were said to equal nearly a third of those on food. Gorbachev evidently decided that the drive to achieve the above-mentioned goals fitted well with his emphasis on economic efficiency. There is no doubt that such provisions, stringently imposed, could pose a serious threat to employment among the country's many heavy drinkers and less assiduous toilers. Ironically, the sale of vodka was for decades encouraged on account of the benefits it brought to the state treasury; but this policy was recently reversed, and the price of vodka increased considerably.

Stricter discipline was embodied in the rules regulating labor within enterprises promulgated in July 1984. Failure to perform prescribed duties, unauthorized absence from one's job, and inebriation at the workplace were dealt with very severely. Managements were empowered to reprimand anyone found guilty, and if necessary transfer him or her to lower-level or lower-paid work for three months. Systematic violation of work rules, absence without permission for more than three hours, or appearance at work in a drunken state could, if combined with a history of bad service, bring about dismissal.[35]

It may well be that these measures provoke widespread resentment, but they may also have contributed to the modest improvements in labor productivity claimed during the first years of the Twelfth Five-Year Plan. Heavy drinking and indiscipline are not the monopoly of the poorer toilers, although such evils undoubtedly promote poverty.

Some Early Results

The social effect of the new policies is as yet unclear, but the prospects for change in employment patterns are vast. The economist Nikolai Shmelev expressed the opinion that in terms of quality only 7–18 percent of Soviet industrial production was up to international standards, which implied that there was enormous scope for reorganization. Another observer, L. Bunich, stated that the imposition of proper economic responsibility would show, for example, that 10 percent of the machine-building plants belonging to the

USSR's Ministry of Chemistry were scarcely viable, or working at a planned loss. Branches of industry such as coal mining, and house construction, and some subbranches, such as lumbering and certain types of urban transport, were, in his view, completely uneconomic.[36]

What can happen to employment levels when efficiency is improved has been illustrated in several other sources. A detailed article on the reorganization of transport in White Russia revealed that by November 1986 dismissals among railway workers had reached 13 percent of the labor force; that the Minsk underground railway had lost 17.9 percent of its staff; and that the air transport administration planned to release 7.6 percent of its work force. Those dismissed tended to work in "less prestigious jobs done mainly by pensioners." In all the cases mentioned, there were substantial pay increases for those who remained. One wonders how divisive Gorbachev's employment policies are likely to be. According to another specialist source, reforms in Estonia resulted in the release of 5 percent of the work force in industry and transport. There was apparently no problem with re-employment, and the whole process was depicted as economically healthy.[37]

An authoritative overview, published in September 1987, claimed that a 10 percent shake-out of labor had been achieved in industry, but that this would fall to 4–5 percent in the period of the current five-year plan. In absolute figures this meant four or five million individuals, at least half of whom would be in employable age groups. Up to that time, 60–80 percent of the workers dismissed in the machine-building industry had been redeployed in the same enterprises.[38] It is hazardous to draw any conclusions on so frail a basis, but the statement would suggest an unemployment level, as a consequence of such policies, of around a million by 1990. This, of course, would be considered very low by capitalist standards.

Another element of uncertainty about employment prospects, and the matters dealt with in this section, is introduced by the disappointing progress of the labor reform itself. Final judgment must be reserved, though, until after 1988, when, according to plan, all productive enterprises are to go over to full self-financing. With regard to new, more effective working practices, some 41 percent of industrial workers were reported to be organized in brigades by 1987, but only 11 percent of the brigades had switched to contractual agreements. Research in a number of enterprises that were supposed to have gone over to self-financing in January of the same year showed that 40 percent of the work force could not name any significant change, while in some cases production indexes had even fallen. Attestation was only two-thirds complete, and the proposed change to multishift working was far behind schedule.[39]

Preparations are nevertheless going ahead to help with redeployment, when it becomes necessary. (The Soviet bureaucracy always seems to react with some ease in cases where new administrative powers have to be established.) Naturally enough, the system of employment bureaus, founded in 1966 and run by local soviets, is being adapted to meet extra demands on their services. These bureaus were formerly concerned with the provision of information on vacancies, and by the beginning of this decade were apparently handling around three million applications annually.

According to a decree published on 19 January 1988, the bureaus are now to work on a self-financing, commercial basis, charging fees to the enterprises they serve. They still, however, must ensure that the people whom they place are aware of, and receive, the various redundancy benefits stipulated by law. The bureaus have been empowered regularly to issue information bulletins and computerize their placement activities. This last function, however, promises to have a darker side: several reports have already shown that the militia and local passport offices have been given access to the data banks for the investigation of persons unemployed for three months or more. The nature of Soviet governance perhaps made this inevitable.[40]

Under the terms of the new decree, the bureaus are to direct applicants primarily into the consumer-goods industries, paid services, subordinate agricultural enterprises, and housing services, and to enterprises in Siberia and on the geographical periphery of the USSR. Obviously, the jobs on offer will be the worst paid, least prestigious, and toughest in the economy. In view of this, recourse to the services of the bureaus must be an unwelcome prospect for many. In the short run Gorbachev's labor policies cannot be implemented without causing hardship.

I cannot conclude this brief survey, however, on too negative a note. Some insecurity of employment may not be a bad thing. The amount of unemployment anticipated is evidently not large and, given the condition of the Soviet economy, need not be of long duration. The slow movement of the reform will itself assist social adjustment. Although the new law on state enterprises affords workers less protection of the traditional type, it does lay more emphasis than hitherto on managerial responsibility for social services—housing, child care, school support, vocational training, and help for pensioners. The code word for all of this is the "human factor."

Help for the Underprivileged

The question of assistance for people who cannot work is hardly less important than the income of those who can. Thus current policies in this sphere also require examination. Soviet planning literature has long made provision for categories of citizens who are most likely to suffer particular hardship, including pensioners of various kinds, members of large or broken families, parentless children, and women who, though employed, bear the burden of pregnancy or dependent children. The Twelfth Five-Year Plan in fact listed a number of undertakings regarding improved social assistance for some of these cases.

The pension system naturally occupies a central place in any scheme of state aid, the categories of persons normally covered being the aged or retired, invalids, and dependents. In the USSR, the existing pension law was introduced by Khrushchev in 1956, at the time when he began to modify the wage structure. Although the payments and thresholds have been changed many times, and are somewhat bewildering in their complexity, the principles of pensionability have remained simple and largely unaltered. Payments are made as a right and are, when possible, employment-related and noncontributory.

The last major change in the system before Gorbachev's advent to power was the introduction, in 1981, of a minimum retirement pension of 50 rubles per month for workers and employees. These, however, were "full" pensions, and persons who had not clocked up the necessary service record, or who were members of collective farms, received less. The Twelfth Five-Year Plan promises another rise in minimum rates, but improvements effected up to the time of writing have taken other forms. Improved minima may, of course, be built into the proposed new pension law, which we shall consider in a moment.[41]

Gorbachev has not shown any special interest in social security, but the main modifications that have been made since he came to power are noteworthy. The first was the increase of monthly payments to 30 rubles for the relatively small number of persons who are not entitled to a formal retirement pension and receive small maintenance payments instead. Enacted in May 1985, this law benefits those who have inadequate service records, and who cannot claim invalid or dependents' pensions. The May law also raised the collective farmers' minimum retirement pension to 40 rubles and allowed local soviets to make small allowances to pensioners "in acute need," providing the personal income of such persons did not exceed 50 rubles a month.

Another, no doubt welcome, change was the introduction, in November 1985, of a mechanism for augmenting retirement pensions as the years went by. The problem here lay in the traditional practice of fixing pensions in accordance with some former earnings, whereas the wage paid for a given job would generally rise with time. Thus people retiring successively from the same job would get ever larger pensions, but all would inevitably suffer from the march of inflation. The new measure applied to pensions that had been started at least ten years previously, and permitted some modest incrementation, at a rate equivalent to 1 percent of the former wage annually. The change affected two levels of monthly pensions only: those under 60 rubles, and those paid on former earnings of over 120 rubles. It meant that most of the help available was directed to the poorest pensioners, on the one hand, and those who had suffered the greatest fall in income on the other. The exigencies of life expectancy, however, must have limited increases to a few rubles in most cases.[42]

In May 1986, a 15 percent penalty for pensioners who continued to work a household garden plot was abolished. Persons who had stayed at the same enterprise for the duration of their pensionable service were allowed to claim an increase of 20 percent, instead of 10 percent as before. Something was also done for registered invalids. In January 1987 their basic pension rates were raised (the new minima ranging from 30–50 rubles a month, according to age and category of disablement), and some free transport was made available. Contrary to popular belief in the West, dispensed medicines are not free in the USSR; pensioners now benefit from a reduction of 50 percent in the charges for them.

These changes, as may be appreciated, were all rather cautious, and the new minima far from generous. By the late 1980s, 50 rubles per month, for example, could cover only part of the living costs of even the most frugal individual. Presumably, the improvements reflected both the considered capability of the state treasury and the obligations anticipated from the aging of the population; between 1980 and 1986 the total number of pensioners of all kinds increased from 50.2 to 56.8 million. No wonder that the present leadership has carefully maintained the policy, initiated in 1979, of encouraging pensioners to continue working after retirement age. At the time of writing, the consequences of all these measures, in terms of improved well-being, can scarcely be judged, as censorship restrictions on pensioners' income still impede assessment.[43]

The configuration of the whole pension system is currently under discussion in preparation for the formulation and enactment of the new pension law. Let us take, by way of illustration, the proposals made by A. Solov'ev, deputy head of the Social Security Division of the USSR State Committee for Labor and Social Questions. His comment is obviously authoritative, and much of what he wrote departed markedly from long-standing practice.[44]

People who had worked for 40 years, he said, enjoyed the same pension entitlement as those who had worked only 25, which was blatantly unfair. The Soviet Union had relatively low retirement thresholds, and the new law evidently envisaged no change in them. But these might advantageously be raised; for example, some people argued that women should normally retire at the same age as men. Perhaps the payment of pensions to persons who continued to work (a policy pursued since the late 1950s) should be discontinued, since it could lead to inflated incomes. On the other hand, the maximum pension rate of 120 rubles per month was very old and caused unhealthy leveling of postretirement income; hence it should become adjustable. The gap between the sums received by urban pensioners and those given to rural pensioners needed review (though Solov'ev did not say in which direction it should be narrowed). Pensions should continue to be 50–60 percent of wage rates, but the possibility of allowing workers to make voluntary contributions should also be considered. The main drift of Solov'ev's proposals was clearly toward a harsher system, more closely tied to earnings over longer years, and certainly more differentiated. This is well and truly in the spirit of the Gorbachev reform.

Other aspects of the social security system have also been subject to change, but we shall mention only the most important here. The laws are in any case very complex and hardly lend themselves to simple commentary. In January 1986, widows who had children formerly ineligible for dependents' pensions acquired the same rights to state aid as single mothers. A decree passed in October set 20 rubles a month as the minimum maintenance allowance payable by a responsible parent for each child left in someone else's care; formerly rates varied from a quarter to a half of the parental salary, with no minimum stipulated. In February 1987, young couples were relieved of income-tax payments during the first year of wedlock.[45]

A number of improvements envisaged in the Twelfth Five-Year Plan were still awaited at the beginning of 1988. With regard to child benefits in families with a per capita income below 50 rubles a month (or 75 rubles in certain inhospitable regions), the plan promised to raise the age for termination of payment from eight to twelve. The benefit was apparently to be left at a mere twelve rubles a month per child, however. Pregnant women who worked and mothers with small or sick children were promised longer leave. More funds were to be made available for catering in preschool institutions, and also for catering and medicine in hospitals and old people's homes, where, incidentally, standards have been described as deplorable.

It is worthy of note that the changes listed here, though genuine enough, were not an integral part of the plan but were stipulated as being "in accordance with it." Apart from the relatively modest levels of improvement so far registered, the proposed timing is disappointing. Implementation was promised "during 1986–1990 and over the period up to 2000." There was no indication of what would be done first, or of who would have to wait until the end of the century—this sensitive matter being left to the discretion of the USSR Council of Ministers. Finally, the policies did not include any advance toward what is termed "national assistance" in the United Kingdom, that is, automatic state aid for people whose income is below a recognized level. This has remained a serious gap in an otherwise reasonably comprehensive system.

Rural Policies Reconsidered

There is little doubt that Gorbachev took an active part in shaping Soviet rural policies long before he assumed the general-secretaryship of the CPSU. By 1970 he was first secretary of the agriculturally important Stavropol' Krai party committee, and from November 1978 on he ran the Department of Agriculture in the Central Committee. This presumably explains why so many of the policies now being pursued in the village were actually launched before he became general secretary.[46]

His public utterances on rural society have been primarily within the context of increasing agricultural production, as envisaged by the May 1982 Food Program and subsequent legislation. The most important administrative changes now promoted include more economic independence for the farm itself; the use of production contracts between farm members and managements; the encouragement of private farming on the household plot; and certain improvements in labor and social-security conditions. These policies, of course, bear a close resemblance to those operative in the industrial sector.

Significantly, Gorbachev has never mooted the possibility of abolishing the collective farm system as such. Indeed, the new January 1988 draft statute defines it as "an integral part of Soviet socialist society." The collective-farm peasantry, as a class, has in recent years been declining in numbers much more slowly than hitherto, and by 1987 still made up 12 percent of the population, or half of the permanent agricultural labor force (most of the rest being state-farm workers). The Soviet leadership may well have decided that, although the collective farm is an unsatisfactory base for modern agriculture, the present rural situation and peasant attitudes toward the land preclude its mass abolition.[47]

As for peasant living standards, the collective-farm income distributed among the farms' members over recent years, in money and kind, seems to have risen impressively. Between 1980 and 1986 members' income from the public sector was said to have grown by no less than 34.1 percent, equaling 159 rubles a month. This improvement was much greater than that for workers and employees. The claimed rises in income were apparently accompanied by improvements in trade, house building, and the provision of school facilities. One must bear in mind, however, that the village was still very backward relative to the towns in the late 1970s. Thus, even when the additional income from the household plot was taken into account, the peasant remained significantly worse off than the average worker or employee.

Beyond this, there is evidence that farm incomes, like those in industry, became more differentiated. Thus, while the average rate of pay for all collective-farm personnel rose by 27 percent during the Eleventh Five-Year Plan, the rates for specialists, technicians, and milkmaids rose by 36 percent, and those of husbandry brigade leaders by 34 percent. In terms of simple arithmetic, this must have lowered the average rise in pay for the less skilled.[48]

Farm Management and Production Contracts

The 1934 and 1969 collective-farm statutes were very restrictive of farm activities. The farm basically was required to fulfill production plans that were prescribed from above, and it had almost no economic independence. Its labor force was regarded as a passive, if essential, element in the scheme, to be directed rather than encouraged. Under the terms of the 1988 statute, which crystallizes the thinking of recent years, the farm is to acquire a new character.[49] The emphasis is moved from plan fulfillment to achieving a substantial increase in agricultural production and selling it. The farm management is to have more freedom to organize production, acquire land or equipment, and fix farm prices (once the traditional state deliveries have been met). Not least important, from the peasantry's point of view, is the drive to replace the old administratively imposed labor obligations and rewards with a freer and more attractive system of internal production contracts and incentives.

The collective-farm statutes of 1934 and 1969 made no mention of any contractual agreements between farm labor and managements. Of course, different kinds of work groups had functioned in both state and collective farms, and very limited contractlike arrangements may have been tolerated in certain collectives. But given the Stalinist nature of the collective farm, proper authorization of such agreements was out of the question. The decree of September 1977, which made their authorization possible, thus represented a startling change of policy. In January 1981 the use of "standardized" contracts was proposed. The new statute goes even further and terms contractual agreements (*podryad*) to be "the main form of production relationship" on the revitalized collective farm. Ideally, they are to form the basis of the new, production-oriented organization and ensure the enthusiastic involvement of the labor force. The peasant is to be freed of constraints that have bound him, in one way or another, since the early 1930s.

Podryad in agriculture was usually envisaged as a family, collective, or brigade arrangement, though individuals could also conclude them. Significantly, in the state farms the old brigade system was strengthened by a decree of May 1982 that stipulated that the new "*podryad* brigades" could be granted long-term responsibility for a particular sector of farm work. State-farm directors were to acquire broader rights in distributing earnings, to better reflect labor inputs; and there was to be more flexibility in paying workers in kind. Payment within the brigade was to be differentiated on the basis of the "coefficient of labor participation," as in other production environments. The decree proposed that collective farms should, where possible, follow the same practices. The parallels with what the government was trying to do in industry are obvious.[50]

Local authorities evidently did their best to encourage the introduction of *podryad*. By 1985 some 39 percent of all agricultural workers on collective and state farms were, it was reported, employed in brigades or the smaller "link" units functioning on a contractual basis and producing 54 percent of the gross agricultural output. The initial object of the *podryad* was, of course, to improve output; but the implementation of such a policy could, if successful, revitalize working relationships throughout the collective farm. It had the potential to enhance not only the economic independence, but also the social status and self-image of the peasant family.[51] The inevitable success stories, were, however, soon followed by ample evidence of disappointing outcomes.

In a critical article published in May 1987, the economist B. Bashmachnikov stated that, although over eleven million agricultural personnel were by then working under contract, with 75 percent of the pastureland and 60 percent of the nation's cattle in their care, the results were "less than they should be." The main reasons were: the difficulty of adapting extensive farming methods to small-group control; formal, as opposed to substantive, switchovers; and the unwillingness of local agricultural officials to permit any really independent economic relationships. Such opposition sprang, of course, from the suspicion that the administrative apparatus could only lose from them. Bashmachnikov also mentioned the tendency for managements to undermine the potential effectiveness of the incentive system by leveling income among brigade members without keen regard for labor inputs. One may presume that, as with most economic reforms, progress was fastest where vested interests were best satisfied.

The Household Plot

The household (or private) plot has always been very important in the collective-farm economy, sometimes saving the peasantry from starvation. It has traditionally provided a significant part of their diet, together with large quantities of meat, vegetables, and fruit for public sale. Official policy toward this sector has been subject to changes that are well documented and scarcely require mention here. Stalin, of course, was intensely hostile to the household plot, and Khrushchev, though relaxing pressures, continued to discourage private agriculture. Only in the late 1970s, as a consequence of continuing supply difficulties, did official attitudes become more positive.

An effective reorientation was signaled by the decree of September 1977, to which we have just referred. This decree stated unequivocally that the "full use of household plots by collective farmers, workers, employees and other people for the production of meat, milk, eggs, potatoes, vegetables, fruit and other agricultural produce is of great importance." To facilitate development, the decree allowed farm administrations, besides signing production contracts with families and individuals, to give plot holders help in acquiring light agricultural machinery, extra livestock, and seed. They were also to assist in marketing, and even the granting of financial assistance. Furthermore, the cultivation of allotments of land was to be encouraged among members of the public.

Other measures of similar import were to follow. The detailed decree of January 1981, noting the current lack of success in promoting the working of household plots, greatly extended the backing that the farm could give in the form of equipment and advances. A few days later an all-union edict reduced restrictions on the use of private plots for growing fodder. After May 1986 (as we have also noted), pensioners working full-sized plots were no longer liable to have their pension reduced. In June 1987 purchasers of empty houses in the countryside were allowed to work the attached plots, and in July local soviets were encouraged to increase the norms for cattle holding, fodder, and pasturage applying to household plots. The terms of the 1988 statute seem to extend this liberal approach: peasants will now be entitled to grow any crops not prohibited by law, build greenhouses, and lease additional land from the farm management. All of which is supposed to inculcate more positive attitudes in the peasants.[52]

The terms of much legislation, however, and the few statistics available, indicate that here, too, results have been at best mixed. Between 1981 and 1987 the size of cattle holdings stagnated or declined, though there was some improvement in the efficiency of production. State purchases of potatoes and vegetables, mostly from the private sector, fell between 1986 and 1987 and were below the average figures for the Eleventh Five-Year Plan. Purchases of fruit were also down, though the authorities could have drawn some consolation from the fact that the 1986 yields were exceptional and better than those of 1985. Agricultural output, of course, must vary somewhat according to the weather, and real change can only be evaluated over a number of seasons. Figures on the proportion of peasant income from the household plot—which is a fairly good overall index—showed that it dropped from 24.7 percent of the family budget in 1980 to 23.1 percent in 1986.[53]

We have found no comprehensive study of the reasons for this sad state of affairs, but commentators usually list, in addition to administrative bottle-necks, the physical difficulties of increasing output, the peasants' rising standard of living (which lessens the attraction of working the household plot), and housing policies tending to concentrate villagers in urban-type flats. On another plane, the economist G. Shmelev indicated that household plots may indeed serve as a useful source of produce, but that to do so they require massive support from the state sector in the form of roads, loans of equipment, fertilizer, pasturage, and so on. This support, and not a questionable ideological foundation, represents the true limits of development of private agriculture.

Moreover, the success of some households, if too conspicuous, could introduce unwanted tensions into an otherwise cohesive collective. Other reports suggested that family agriculture worked best where there were unused facilities for housing animals, as in depopulated villages, or in large, underemployed families, predominantly in Islamic regions. Attempts to introduce family contracts based on household plots in the Moscow oblast, for example, apparently failed. Continuing difficulties in reinvigorating agriculture go some way to explaining why the drive to increase private and collective allotments worked by the public has been so successful: by 1985 nearly twelve million families, urban as well as rural, were involved.[54]

Conditions of Agricultural Labor and Other Matters

The changes in the sphere of labor law are best considered in the form they assumed in the 1988 charter, since this document neatly summarizes many relatively recent enactments and updates rights and duties.

The most sensitive question in the recent history of the peasantry is arguably that of farm membership. The 1934 statute did not envisage formal application for admission; thus peasant children were, by implication, born into their jobs. Happily, this situation was modified in 1969, and a procedure was introduced for applying to join the farm at the age of sixteen. The 1988 version understandably left that unchanged. Voluntary departure from the farm, on the other hand, was not permitted either in the 1934 or the 1969 law, the main task being, from the official point of view, to keep people on the land, unless they could be usefully directed into work elsewhere. In 1988, though, there was a significant legal breakthrough, in that the peasant, at long last, acquired "the right to leave the farm" by means of a written application presented three months in advance of departure. So ended a restriction that cast a shadow on Soviet reality for over 40 years.

Labor discipline on collective farms has always been a problem, exacerbated by low pay and alcoholism. Some solution to the common unwillingness to work in the public fields is being sought in the reorientation of farm management and in the contract system. But apart from this, the new statute retains a strict, paternalistic stance and includes sanctions that, although not new, resemble closely those operative in nonagricultural enterprises. The new formulation reads: "Members of the farm who without good reason fail to put in the established minimum of labor in the public sector, who are guilty of lax working or failure to appear, including an absence of more than three hours without good cause, or appearance at work in a drunken state, those who leave the farm without good reason before the end of the agricultural year, and also those who have been excluded by a decision of the board, supported by other members, can be partially or completely deprived of extra pay, bonuses, and other material incentives." Financial responsibility for damage to farm property is increased from one-third to the whole of one month's average wage. The general meeting of members also retains the right to expel anyone who does not fulfill his duties, although there is a new clause giving unfairly dismissed kolkhozniks the right to claim up to three months' pay as compensation.

Guaranteed monthly payments for collective-farm members (at levels approved by the farm) were introduced in 1966, and regarded, again, as a step toward improving the gap in pay between worker and peasant. Significantly, this provision finds no precise reflection in the 1988 statute, and seems to be overridden by the farm's right to fix its own rates of pay, depending on the final results of productive activities. "Guaranteed pay for members," we now find, "is ensured by extended production, the receipt of a planned net income and the conscientious fulfillment of labor obligations." Nor is there any specific reference to a minimum wage for peasants.

The last matter, however, has recently provoked some public comment. Referring to the gradual introduction of the 80-ruble minimum in state institutions, the economist P. Pushkarenko wrote:

> As for the collective farms, they follow such changes as well as their economies allow . . . The collective farms in the Ukraine, for example, apply tariff rates that were operative in state farms earlier, and that guaranteed different minimum-wage rates. Differentiation takes place not only between farms, but also inside them . . . Mechanizers, persons working in animal husbandry, administrative and office staff have a guaranteed wage level that matches current state-farm rates, but collec-

tive farmers in unmechanized jobs have another level, which is lower. For this reason, it is extremely important to introduce everywhere the [same] guaranteed minimum wage that was established for workers and employees in state farms.[55]

The 1988 charter also reflects recent developments in the sphere of social security. It is well known that rank-and-file members of the collective farm were for many years prohibited from joining the agricultural workers' trade union, and excluded from such benefits as it could offer (representation at managerial level, access to holiday facilities, better protection of labor and social-security rights, and so on). In the early 1970s, however, this policy was changed, and by the end of the decade the overwhelming majority of farm members were unionized. Perhaps not surprisingly, the new version of the charter makes several references to the protective functions of the farm union committee, including its role in settling labor disputes. Further, in a section devoted to the social development of the farm, we find references to the implementation of recent legislation benefiting working women, juveniles, and families. New also are references to the need to reduce heavy physical labor, provide homes for old people, and help with housing on the farm itself; and there is to be more cooperation than hitherto with the local soviets.

It is worth noting, in conclusion, that the establishment of departments of the State Committee for Labor and Social Questions in rural soviets in 1984 integrates with these changes. The departments are to effect outside supervision over matters of labor, pay, social security, farm-supported amenities, child care, catering, and schools. The work of these departments has been little documented in published sources, but the economic independence now proposed for agricultural enterprises may, paradoxically, increase their importance: the state authorities must, after all, retain adequate instruments of inspection and intervention.[56]

Most of the rural policies now being implemented were started well before their industrial counterparts and are no less ambitious. Here, too, the social impact, and probable end results are by no means clear. According to plan, living standards are to rise more quickly than in the towns. The extension of the contract system would, however, favor the farms and peasants whose production prospects were better anyway. As for the household plot, Soviet writers seem to believe it is of greater importance to peasants involved in unskilled, low-paid work. On the face of it, then, one would expect those groups to benefit. Yet the plots that are likely to prosper most from Gorbachev's policies are those that are well situated for marketing, or that were well-developed before. The encouragement of personal initiative must, of course, help some peasants, but its main thrust is likely to favor the strongest and, again, encourage economic differentiation.[57]

The measures comprise a mixture of limited, but realistic benefits balanced by steely requirements for more individual effort. The peasantry is being treated more subtly than it has been since the distant days of Lenin's New Economic Policy. How far the measures will be implemented, and how people will respond to them, must remain another subject of conjecture.

Democratization and Poverty Interests

In the preceding pages, my main concern has been to examine the social policies of the Gorbachev leadership with particular reference to material well-being. Yet, man does not live by bread alone, and some reference must be made here to the matter of political reform. Politics are not only a factor in their own right; they closely intermesh with most other aspects of social existence. Politics and social problems are rarely far apart.

The key word in this sphere is *democratization*. The period between Gorbachev's advent to power and the nineteenth Party Conference of July 1988 saw ever bolder reference to it. We may well enquire which of the proposals made so far are most likely to affect the man in the street. Even if the plans are implemented, proper assessment of their impact will, again, take time; for genuine political change and social responses to it are not easily measured. A few generalizations, however, need to be made at this juncture.

Structural changes are proposed in virtually all major public organizations, but most of the proposals aired so far bear on the CPSU, economic enterprises and organizations, and the hierarchy of soviets. Other institutions, including the Komsomol and the trade unions, will follow suit, if and when the reforms proceed.

Of all types, the most sensitive is certainly the party. In his speech to the January 1987 plenum of the Central Committee, Gorbachev made two specific suggestions, namely, that voting for secretaries of party organizations up to the level of the union republic should be secret, which would allow relatively safe opposition to candidates, and that party members should be allowed to write in extra candidates on their voting paper, which would broaden popular choice. It is difficult to see, however, how such proposals could be brought in without undermining the all-important *nomenklatura* system. As subsequent press comment showed, they hardly had any effect on the first round of internal party elections that followed them.[58]

A decree of the nineteenth Party Conference went further, and called (among other things) for a limited five-year term of office for elected officials, regular changes in the membership of party committees, and a reduction in the size of the permanent apparatus. Party members were to take a more active role in running party affairs; there was to be more openness and a more imaginative admissions policy.

Yet it is arguable that, even if fully implemented, such measures will have little immediate effect in the social sphere. The CPSU has always aimed to garner the most active and responsible toilers in each and every Soviet establishment, and thereafter protect their interests. Candidates for membership in the party are, therefore, not usually underprivileged; in fact, the contrary is true. Further, involvement in the CPSU brings it own material rewards, and given the nature of deficits in consumer goods, it is difficult to see a new ethic emerging quickly. Indeed, increased emphasis on rewards, and promotion by result, as demanded by the current leadership, would appear to make admission to party ranks more difficult for unsuccessful toilers. It is not easy to imagine a "poverty lobby" forming in the average organization, or a significant influx of officials keenly motivated by considerations of social justice. No figures, to our knowledge, have been published on members' earnings, but such poverty as exists among them is probably confined to up-and-coming young specialists, and to party pensioners.

With regard to the election and confirmation of managerial staff, all toilers, regardless of earnings, should have a vote as the new enterprise law is adopted. In this case it is quite possible to imagine different groups of workers having conflicting interests, and favoring candidates with different priorities. People on lower incomes would presumably vote so as to promote policies most likely to enlarge their wage packets in the short, rather than long, term. Highly skilled workers might favor the path of technological change that could take time, or be disadvantageous to the less skilled. Poor families are more dependent on the facilities provided from the enterprise social funds, such as cheap catering and child care, and might be more swayed than others by these considerations. The history of Soviet economic management, however, makes it most unlikely that overtly divisive situations will be allowed to occur. The internal cohesion of the working class is, after all, a prime tenet of Marxism-Leninism, and the apparatus would not welcome instability in the choice of key figures. The prospects of success for these election reforms are not, at present, bright.

From the point of view of solving problems of deprivation, the most promising changes are those promised in the hierarchy of soviets. A decree following the twenty-seventh Party Congress granted citizens some choice of candidate in elections to the local soviets. The "people's deputies" have, of course, little power of legislative initiative or protest, and most of their activities are rather formal. Complaints about the sloppy or ineffective conduct of deputies' meetings have been common for years. They are obliged, however, to maintain a fair amount of direct contact with their constituents. If an effective choice of candidate is really placed before the voters, and if the deputies elected are allowed to adopt differing stances with regard to local issues, we may well find some embryonic form of poverty lobby coming into being.

The first indications, alas, have not been promising. In the very small number of trial constituencies (only some 4 percent), in the Russian Soviet Federated Socialist Republic local elections of June 1987, the unsuccessful candidates did not disappear from view, but were given a reserve status. This presumably gave them some standing, despite their defeat, and kept them in line for future use. The traditional variety of *nomenklatura*-based control from above, to the exclusion of unacceptable local interests, may easily be maintained in this manner. The best advantage that the less privileged people might derive from the new practice would perhaps be a greater sensitivity of some candidates to issues pertaining to poverty and more freedom to speak out about them.

Here, however, the nineteenth Party Conference has prepared the ground for more change, which, if executed, could at last make the soviets as a whole more effective in solving social problems. The proposed reform of the Supreme Soviet may result in the formation of a more effective body, meeting in frequent session and under a national president elected by secret voting. In the localities, full-time administrators may lose their status as deputies (and with it the power to influence sessions of the soviet in their favor). Elected deputies are urged to play a proper role in solving local issues and exercise more control over the apparatus.[59]

Gorbachev's social reforms, aimed at revitalizing Soviet society, are on the whole imaginative and, within the constraints of Soviet reality, worthy of some admiration. They are at least designed to make that society somewhat more open and flexible. Yet by the summer of 1988, the chances of success were at best mixed. In most of the spheres we have examined progress was slow and disappointing. The long-term economic difficulties seemed to preclude rapid improvement in living standards. The promotion of contractual relations and incentive schemes, in both industry and agriculture, together with the modest expansion of private enterprise, had run into difficulties. Differentiation of income, which could bring positive results in contemporary Soviet society, was also way behind schedule. The mood among intellectuals and throughout the country as a whole was restive and disappointed.

In such circumstances, it would be too much to expect massive advances in all spheres at once. The less privileged strata of society could well benefit from the new policies in the end—if they are successful. But people are promised, in the medium term, a harsher and more competitive social climate. The problems of Soviet society are great, and my assessment of progress so far is not too encouraging. For the time being, it might even be said that the most promising element of government policy was the *glasnost'* campaign, which did, at least, promise more awareness of social difficulties, and constructive debate about solving them.

2 | Soviet Living Standards and Consumer Reactions

Measures of Shortage, Expectation, and Satisfaction

Introduction

Despite the emphasis on moral incentives that has characterized official utterances in the Soviet Union over the last seven decades, the Soviet citizen seems to have retained vigorous acquisitive urges. The chronic shortages of goods which have so far proved insurmountable, the materialistic orientation of Marxism-Leninism, and the proclaimed need to catch up with the West, have probably strengthened them.

There have been times when reference to ignoble, consumerist matters was virtually banned from the Soviet media. We may search the Stalinist press in vain for objective reference to low pay, endless queues, or desperate overcrowding. The rebirth of Soviet sociology in the early 1960s, however, and the scope subsequently allowed for scholarly criticism, resulted in some investigation not only of what people really wanted, in a material sense, but also of the existing shortages and of the common responses to them. Work of this kind became quite revealing toward the end of the Brezhnev era, predating *glasnost'* by a number of years. My aim in this section is to present some of the more important and interesting findings, incomplete, or a little contradictory, though they may be. The nature of sociological investigation precludes perfection.

A word of caution is, of course, needed at the outset. Satisfaction, or dissatisfaction, is meaningful only in a relative sense. The most obvious points of reference are some ideal state (presumably 100 percent satisfaction in a communist land); a situation obtaining some time in the past; or levels in other societies. Measurement, even in the most favorable conditions, is difficult, as numerous investigations have shown.[1] Levels of satisfaction or dissatisfaction may be affected by numerous factors: age, sex, education, occupation, family commitments, individual moods and expectations, and so on. When the rigors of Soviet censorship are added to all this, the need for care in interpreting Soviet data hardly needs to be stressed. Nevertheless, much honest work goes into collecting them, and the figures produced by the most reliable writers may be taken as genuinely indicative of achievements and reactions.

Let us begin our review with evidence on the configuration of elements, material and spiritual, that the respondents in a number of recent sociological surveys declared to be most important in their life-styles. Then we shall go on to consider how far they were satisfied with the prevailing levels of provision of those elements. To make the topic a little more manageable, I shall consider only the principal findings in each case, leaving the reader to peruse the tables for lesser revelations.

The Popular Desire for Material Well-being

The best results that I have located up to the present come from an apparently rather careful study of 4,137 people in Riga and two other small Latvian towns conducted some time after 1979. The aim of the study was to assess family size within the context of what the researchers called "life values"; the ratings of these values across the whole sample are shown in table 2.1. Though the republic of Latvia is unique in many cultural respects, I would argue that in questions of so general a nature it provides a fair measure of public attitude at least in European Russia. The values turned up by the study do not appear to be ideologically slanted, and the patterns for the two sexes are fairly close. Grouping together close results (for such measurement is only approximate anyway) and listing by order of prominence, we find that the respondents had four broad categories of desiderata.

Far and away the highest ratings were given to "family happiness" and "material well-being," in almost equal measure. This finding prompts the simple thought that people are basically the same everywhere. The next two categories, consisting, in the first instance, of work and travel, and in the second, of sociocultural matters, were much less important. Negligible ratings were achieved by sociopolitical activity and "other values," suggesting that the listing was reasonably complete. The authors of the study went on to illustrate changes in the balance of values over a life span, but these changes showed few unexpected features. Most significantly, the concern with material well-being, though strong throughout adulthood, seemed to

Table 2.1   *Average Ratings of "Life Values" by Relative Importance*

Life values	Men	Women
Family happiness	.69	.75
Material sufficiency	.68	.66
Interesting creative work	.36	.37
Success at work	.26	.24
Travel	.26	.27
Knowledge of news	.19	.11
Pleasant company	.19	.20
Artistic pleasure	.17	.25
Eventful life	.13	.11
Physical development	.12	.06
Social activity	.03	.03
Other values	.02	.02
Superiority over others	.01	.01

SOURCE: P. A. Eglite, *Sotsiologicheskie issledovaniia* (hereafter *S. I.*), 1985, no. 4: 60.

NOTE: For an explanation of the methodology the reader is referred to another Latvian publication, *Faktory i motivy demograficheskogo povedeniya* (Riga: Zinatie, 1984). Suffice it to note here that the ratings are comparable and expressed as decimal fractions of unity.

peak in the 20–24-year age group, when it far exceeded interest in family happiness and children.

Such results are a far cry from the old ideological premises about the altruism of Soviet man. But recent years have seen the publication of many studies critical of the official teachings in this sphere. Two young sociologists, for example, won a local sociological prize for a study which demonstrated that "material well-being" was most often given the highest priority through all age groups between 20 and 65 years, and that this priority varied less than others, including even housing, health, interesting work, and the family.[2]

The concept "material well-being" may be stretched to include many distinct elements. An extensive all-union study of the life-styles of Soviet people in 27 towns conducted in 1980–1981 under the leadership of I. T. Levykin provided data on popular evaluation of the relative importance of a number of these elements (table 2.2). Each of the three social groups distinguished— workers, collective farmers, and "intellectuals"—put "material security" together with food and clothing at the top of their listings. Presumably, that concept subsumed income, which may account for the lower rating of

Table 2.2   *Weighting of Elements in Life-Style by Relative Importance*

Elements	Workers	Collective farmers	Intellectuals
Material security	.685	.728	.680
Dress	.685	.706	.695
Food	.645	.728	.680
Leisure, holidays	.623	.561	.599
Free time facilities	.540	.578	.512
Chances of social contact	.499	.558	.500
Environment	.474	.514	.545
Housing conditions	.429	.622	.423
Wage	.409	.578	.507

SOURCE: V. Kh. Bigulov, A. O. Kryshtanovskii, and A. S. Michurin, *S. I.,* 1984, no. 4: 88 (listing rearranged).

NOTE: As for table 2.1, the source lacks a proper explanation of methodology, but the figures are based on Pearson correlations and measure relative importance among the chosen elements. The order of presentation has been changed to facilitate perusal.

"wage." The fact that housing conditions were not thought to be very important is puzzling, given the intensity of the problem in the USSR, but this reading may have been due to untypical sampling. Further perusal of the columns will reveal some interesting differences between the social groups.

More complex is the problem of the degree to which people are satisfied with their living conditions. The most relevant findings in this case come from a standardized survey of five cities (Moscow, Leningrad, Alma-Ata, Kiev, and Baku) conducted within the context of the same all-union study. To ease appreciation of the findings, we have simplified the data and arranged the elements in three categories: personal, environmental, and professional (table 2.3). The Moscow results are shown as separate columns. The categorization of replies only as "good" or "bad" is most disappointing. This may have been done to mask the various degrees of dissatisfaction. Nevertheless, the observable pattern is not without interest.

Over the whole sample, only 34 percent of the respondents declared their "material well-being" to be good, and 7 percent thought it bad. The corresponding figures for "life as a whole" were 52 and 2 percent. Housing, which heads the second group, is here revealed as a problem for many, while most public services were a cause of general dissatisfaction. The best rating was achieved by "work," but wages were clearly a very sore point. Educational facilities were greatly appreciated, and rated as good by no less than

78 percent of respondents in the large towns. It is noteworthy that satisfaction levels among the public in Moscow were, in general, lower, though the provision of goods and services there is undoubtedly better than in most other large towns. This may be taken either as an illustration of improved supplies heightening, rather than satisfying, expectations, or as sociological "proof" of the greater sophistication of Muscovites.

Differences among certain subgroups in the same survey in material well-being, clothes, housing, and leisure facilities were revealed in another article (table 2.4). On the whole, we find that the responses were fairly even. People living in rural areas were more satisfied with their material well-being, food, and clothing, than townsfolk. If, as is generally held, living conditions are

Table 2.3 *Popular Assessments of Living Conditions (percentages of all replies)*

	All large towns		Moscow	
Category	Good	Bad	Good	Bad
Personal				
Material well-being	34	7	23	6
Food	52	3	51	2
Clothing	36	3	27	4
Life as a whole	52	2	44	4
Environmental				
Housing	44	17	42	20
Public services, including:				
Medical care	49	9	44	10
Education for children	78	2	57	4
Catering	26	19	23	20
Amenities	33	14	27	12
Trade (shopping)	20	25	18	—
Transport	30	21	15	36
Culture	39	11	27	12
Opportunities for leisure	43	6	39	8
Professional				
Work	58	2	45	3
Skill, profession	47	3	38	4
Wage	10	14	8	16

SOURCE: O. B. Bozhkov and V. B. Golofast, *S. I.*, 1985, no. 3: 98.

Table 2.4   *Evaluation of Various Factors by Subgroup*
(percentage giving response of "good" on a three-point scale)

Coverage/subgroup	Material well-being	Food	Clothes	Housing	Leisure	Overall
All-union (sample)	37.7	53.3	40.8	43.5	39.3	49.3
Large-town residents	34.1	52.0	36.0	43.5	43.1	51.7
Rural residents	45.4	57.7	49.9	43.7	35.0	54.3
Young people (18–29)	34.4	56.3	44.0	36.3	39.2	54.8

SOURCE: I. T. Levykin, *S. I.*, 1984, no. 2: 94.

worse in the village, we have an interesting contrast with the Moscow results. It may be that villagers are indeed less demanding, and that the marked
improvements of recent years have made them happier with their lot.

Young people appear to be least satisfied with their material well-being
and housing. This may surely be explained by the fact that they tend to be at
the bottom of the pertinent wage scales, and at the wrong end of the local
waiting lists. The author of the article provided other figures, though, showing that between half and three quarters of the respondents (excluding
young people) had noted an improvement in their living conditions over the
preceding five years.

We have considered the results of the all-union survey in a little detail because they are apparently unique in their coverage, and the figures,
though incomplete as published, are the fullest to come to our notice. Not
surprisingly, there is evidence from many smaller studies that dissatisfaction
with living standards is well above the "bad" levels shown in table 2.3. Thus
an investigation of attitudes among young specialists working in the coal-
mining industry in the Ukraine conducted at about the same time showed
21.5–36.8 percent dissatisfaction rates over a similar range of indices, while
some 45–70 percent of the young migrants to the BAM (Baikal-Amur Railway) building sites expressed discontent with the living conditions they
found there.[3] Other information of a similar nature will no doubt be made
available as Gorbachev's proclaimed policy of *glasnost'* progresses.

Satisfaction with Wage Levels

A central factor—perhaps the central factor—in anyone's personal assessment of his standard of living is his or her wage packet. We are fortunate

that the Soviet toilers' attitudes toward their earnings have also become a subject of considerable interest to Soviet sociologists. Given the selflessness that is still, in the sphere of ideology, attributed to Soviet man, the topic is usually treated with caution; nonetheless, much of the collected data is well worthy of attention.

Results from some of the most convincing studies of wage satisfaction that we have been able to find are shown in table 2.5. Although they are not readily comparable, as we know too little about the samples, all reveal significant levels of discontent. The most extensive of them (part of the all-union study) provides two general figures of 14 and 18 percent for dissatisfaction with "wages" and "material incentives." In most of the other cases, though, the figures are considerably higher. The sample of engineers, for example, yields a rate of 81 percent, while the Lenkoran' study, conducted by a local party office, shows surprising levels over all seven occupation groups investigated. The Ryazan' study seems to demonstrate that the rate of dissatisfaction rises steadily as wages shrink. Indeed, all of these samples together justify a firm conclusion of mass dissatisfaction with wage levels. We selected them for their apparent reliability; figures indicating much lower levels of dissatisfaction have not been deliberately excluded, or, in fact, found. Furthermore, a number of worker-migration studies, whose findings are rather too complex for consideration here, indicate that dissatisfaction with wage levels is a prominent factor in many people's decisions to seek new jobs.[4]

The most analytical single study of satisfaction with wages to come to our notice was conducted in 1977 in the Tuvan ASSR, among a professionally mixed group of ethnic Tuvans. Although this work was intended to illustrate the responses of an urbanized ethnic minority, I imagine that it gives a fairly representative pattern of satisfaction levels in many provincial work forces. It also contained some useful correlatory analysis of the subgroups covered.[5]

The average level of wage dissatisfaction in the sample ("not completely satisfied" and "not satisfied") ranged narrowly from 22−23 percent of the respondents, depending on the subgroup. Levels of dissatisfaction seemed to be almost equal between the sexes, and educational attainment did not seem to affect attitudes very much either (except that fewer respondents in the best educated group—12.6 percent—were dissatisfied). For unexplained reasons, 37 percent of the least educated respondents did not answer the question. Among age groups, replies of "not quite satisfied" peaked at 30−34 years (23.8 percent of the respondents), and "not satisfied" at 40−44 years (9 percent). Possibly, the peaks corresponded with financial demands of the family, or disappointment over an already established career pattern.

In terms of place of residence, wage dissatisfaction was most frequent (30 percent of respondents) in Kyzyl, the capital, and lowest in Ak-dovurak (14.3 percent). As for branches of the economy, it was most common in the

Table 2.5 *Wage-Satisfaction Levels*

Coverage of survey	Percentage of respondents dissatisfied	Definitions (when available)
All-union	18	"material stimulus" inadequate
	14	"work bad"
Urban dwellers, Tuva ASSR	22.4	"not completely satisfied, or dissatisfied"
Specialists in Ukrainian coal industry	24	"dissatisfied"
Leningrad engineers	81	"dissatisfied"
Individual workers in Estonia	36	"dissatisfied with bonuses"
Brigade workers	44	"dissatisfied with bonuses"
Lenkoran' (Azerbaijan) study		
Cultural staff	51.7	"dissatisfied"
Urban teachers	61.4	
Rural teachers	40	
Doctors, nurses	56.6	
State-farm workers	85	
Tin-factory workers	71.9	
Construction workers	71.3	
Ryazan' industrial enterprises (workers by wage group)		
75–100 rubles	50.7	"dissatisfied"
101–125	45.9	
126–150	37.8	
151–175	36.7	
176–200	27.8	
201–250	15.9	
251–300	13.0	

SOURCES: (1) Bozhkov and Golofast, p. 97; (2) Boiko, p. 16; (3) Tikhonov, p. 114; (4) Kalinin, p. 96; (5) Luk'ianov, p. 107 (recalculated); (6) Dzhamalova and Batygin, p. 56; (7) Simakov, p. 107. For further details, see the bibliography.

lowest paid: trade, catering, housing, and communal services (the figures for them ranging between 26 and 31 percent). "Administration," entered as a separate branch, registered the lowest figure of all for wage dissatisfaction (10.9 percent of respondents). Perhaps the most curious range, however, was yielded by the socio-occupational groups. Dissatisfaction was most frequent among manual workers doing mechanized jobs (29 percent) and among skilled specialists (23.5 percent); the cultural, service, and skilled workers had rates of around 18 percent.

Another dimension of the problem is how adequate people consider their pay to be in terms of what it has to be spent on. Some answers were provided by T. Z. Protasenko's most interesting study of 1,434 employed persons in Leningrad in 1982–1983. The respondents, aged 26–40, were drawn from four occupational groups (service workers, teachers, engineers, and workers) with average group salaries ranging from 143–203 rubles a month. We suspect that the sample was fairly homogeneous in terms of well-being, because per capita incomes ranged only from 103–112 rubles. The principal findings are nevertheless among the most interesting of their kind to appear.

As may be seen from table 2.6, no less than 7–10 percent of the respondents lived from hand to mouth, while another 30–50 percent had only just enough money to manage on, even purchases of clothes causing difficulty. Interestingly, the service workers again considered themselves to be among the best provided for; a cynical explanation for this would attribute their

Table 2.6 *Personal Assessment of Material Well-Being*
(percentage of respondents in each group)

Assessment	Service workers	Teachers	Engineers	Workers
We live from wage packet to wage packet	9.7	8.8	7.4	10.0
We have enough for daily expenses, but then it is hard; even buying clothes is difficult	31.7	41.9	50.0	34.7
Basically we have enough; we even save sometimes, but big purchases are difficult	44.0	34.9	34.6	47.6
Purchase of durable consumer goods is not difficult, but a car is inaccessible	12.0	12.8	7.4	7.7
In fact we refuse ourselves nothing	2.6	1.6	0.6	–

SOURCE: T. Z. Protasenko, *S. I.*, 1985, no. 3: 105.

assessment of their material well-being to easier access to pilfered or black-market goods. The table may well give a fair assessment of widespread views of pay packets among people earning sums close to the national average. The responses of the low-paid could hardly be less positive. Of course, the low level of what we might call "reserve income" among the great majority of the population is not in doubt. It was well illustrated in the spring of 1987 in an article by the well-known economist Anatolii Aleksandrovich Ovsiannikov. Discussing the findings of a broad survey of 1,500 families in Tomsk in 1983, he demonstrated that the largest group—some 56 percent of the sample—spent 52.3 percent of their money income on food and clothing alone. In addition to this, 16.1 percent went for alcoholic beverages, leaving less than a quarter of their income for services, furnishings, transport, and other purposes.[6]

There is some interesting evidence that the run-of-the-mill assessments of wage satisfaction both underestimate the psychological importance of wages and overestimate public satisfaction with them. A potent mine was thrust under the chariot of Marxist-Leninist ideologues in the form of an unusual study by the sociologists N. M. Popova and V. B. Moin. Writing in February 1983, they claimed that the "traditional" distinction between moral and financial incentives was by no means always justified, because in socialist society wages "perform both functions."[7]

Some people thought sociological investigations proved that people placed labor first among their life values; but such results, said the authors, were incorrectly acquired or interpreted. The high appraisal of moral incentives was exaggerated because respondents tended to give answers they thought were socially acceptable. The gap between what people really thought and the answers they put in questionnaires could be clarified if respondents were asked to assess other people's work motivation alongside their own. This little exercise was duly conducted, and the results turned out to be quite intriguing. As may be seen from table 2.7, respondents were in all cases ready to attribute a far higher degree of mercenary interest to fellow workers than to themselves.

Furthermore, the study found that about a fifth of the respondents contradicted themselves in successive answers, while no less than three-quarters estimated their wage incorrectly, showing a strong tendency toward reduction to average figures from both extremes. The most probable explanation here was that low earnings were thought to indicate indifference to labor or low skill levels, while high earnings were associated with "quick buck" attitudes, or a socially unacceptable concern with material things. The authors ended this rather disturbing article by saying that the fact that "wages did not occupy a proper place in the value system of the workers of a socialist

Table 2.7   *Percentages of Respondents Indicating "Wage" as Motivation for Certain Actions*

	"Rational": applied to respondent	*"Attributed":* applied to others	*Difference in percentages*
Negative act: Leaving work			
Study 1	27	65	38
Study 2	34	86	52
Negative act: Migration from the village			
Study 3	4	39	35
Positive act: Assessing employment			
Studies 2 and 4	9	29	20
Study 5	7	17	10

SOURCE: N. M. Popova and V. B. Moin, *S. I.*, No 2, 1983, no. 2: 106.

NOTE: Few details of the studies were provided, but all were conducted between 1975 and 1982 and involved a total of 4,500 respondents, including: (1) employees of the Black Sea Technical Fleet; (2) employees of the Ilichev Ship-Repair Yard; (3) residents of the Krasnoknyanskii District, Odessa oblast; (4) employees of the Odessa Ship-Repair Yard; and (5) technical personnel of 14 ship-repair yards.

society was an alarming symptom, indicating shortcomings in educative work, and the need for further perfection of the wage system." This, I suggest, was another way of saying that people should be taught not to be ashamed of their earnings, which needed upward adjustment anyway.

Assessment of changes in satisfaction levels over time is not easy, as little comparable work was done in earlier years. Some chronological perspective may, however, be obtained by drawing on labor studies conducted in Leningrad by a group of eminent sociologists in 1962 and again in 1976. These were the most respectable investigations made after the resuscitation of Soviet sociology in the 1960s, and the first of them attracted a certain amount of attention in the West.[8]

The principal focus of the 1962 study, as published, was the job rather than wage satisfaction, and although it touched on wages several times, it avoided the concentration afforded to other matters. Nevertheless, the authors found that over a sample of 2,665 workers, 31.7 percent were dissatisfied with pay, while an almost equal number refrained from expressing an opinion (p. 317). The average wage of "satisfied" workers was then 100 rubles, as against 84 rubles for "dissatisfied" ones. As might be expected, wage dissatisfaction correlated quite closely with job dissatisfaction in general (p. 178).

Simplistic conclusions are to be avoided, and so tenuous a data base prompts particular caution. It would appear, however, that while dissatisfaction with wages was extensive among urban workers in the early 1960s, it did not pass, and may well have spread, over the following two decades. Indeed, most of the serious research on wage satisfaction seems to have produced rather unwelcome results of one kind or another, demonstrating yet again that the problems not only of sufficiency, but also of distribution, still await solution in Soviet society.

Unsatisfied Consumer Demand

Satisfaction with one's life-style depends in no small measure on the quality and availability of goods and services. Such elements in fact form an integrated equation. I have already presented some popular assessments of living conditions as a whole. Something more needs to be said, however, on the shortfalls of consumer goods and services common in the Soviet economy. Despite some progress in satisfying demand in recent years, Soviet society is still characterized by great deficits of consumer goods. The concept of "shortage" is also very relative, but the Soviet leadership appears to measure it with reference to (*a*) certain scientifically based "rational norms," (*b*) what its citizens en masse would like to buy, yet cannot, and (*c*) the standards of plenty in European or capitalist society. As a result of government concern, and the (albeit sporadic) improvements registered through the 1960s and early 1970s, some overt discussion of this problem was permitted even before the *glasnost'* campaign started. Let us look at some of the clearer evidence available to date.

As already noted, the shortages are to some extent perceptible as a macroeconomic problem in the published statistical sources. It is no secret, for example, that branch "B" of the economy (that producing consumption goods) has frequently underperformed; that wages in some sectors (and hence demand) have grown faster than productivity; that personal savings have increased considerably, which suggests an inadequate supply of goods; and that the gap between state prices and the "free" prices charged on the collective-farm market has recently widened. On the other hand, stocks of unsold and unsellable goods are an ongoing problem. Soviet sources contain, of course, many references to these failings. More specific measures of shortfall for particular items or services may sometimes be obtained by comparing data of different provenance.

Shortfalls in Food, Clothing, and Household Goods

The best measure of such shortfalls to be published takes the form of gaps between the average provision and the "rational norms" for food, clothing, and household goods. Table 2.8 brings together some available figures in an attempt to illustrate this for foodstuffs. The table shows that by 1984 the deficit of fruit and berries was still very great, while the supplies of meat, vegetables, and milk products were also much below needed levels. In contrast, consumption of bread and sugar significantly exceeded the norms for them. Improvement between 1970 and 1984 was, on the whole, slow and unsteady. Given the dubious quality of much Soviet produce (and the possible inflation of statistics), I think it likely that the real shortfalls were greater. Indeed, evidence from non-Soviet sources strongly supports this suspicion. For example, surveys by Radio Free Europe/Radio Liberty of food availability have now been conducted among recent Soviet emigrés for a number of years. Of the 1,269 people who participated in the survey conducted between January 1984 and March 1985, only 5–10 percent said that meat was regularly available for purchase in the place where they had resided. With regard to milk, cheese, and tomatoes, 47, 26, and 16 percent, respectively, of the respondents said these foods had been regularly available.[9]

Table 2.8 *Per Capita Consumption of Food as Percentage of "Rational Norms"*

	Per capita consumption (%)			"Rational norm," 1983 (kilos)
Product groups	1970	1980	1984	
Meat and meat products	60.9	73.8	77.4	78
Milk and milk products	75.8	77.5	78.3	405
Eggs [units]	54.4	81.8	87.7	292
Fish and fish products	84.6	96.7	96.1	18.2
Fruit and berries	38.5	41.8	49.5	91
Vegetables, pulses	63.1	74.6	79.2	130
Potatoes	118.2	99.1	100.0	110
Butter	74.7	96.7	105.5	9.1
Bread products	129.6	120.0	117.4	115
Sugar	97.0	111.0	111.0	40

SOURCES: A. I. Levin and N. M. Rimashevskaia, *S. I.*, 1983, no. 1: 46; *Narodnoe khozyaistvo SSSR v 1984*, p. 459.

As for clothing, the per capita consumption figures for cloth and certain garments may be compared with a set of rational norms quoted by Iurii A. Gusev (table 2.9). It would appear that the deficits of clothing were on the whole greater than those of foodstuffs; supplies of footwear, perhaps not surprisingly, came closest to adequacy. Improvements over the same period were likewise slow. The picture presented on the basis of Gusev's categories is not complete, since he omits a figure for artificial fibers; in Soviet statistical sources, as we know, omission is all too often a sign of malaise.

A set of "rational" holdings of other consumer durables, particularly household goods, has not, to our knowledge, been published, but desirable levels would presumably approach saturation point in the space available, minus an allowance for households that did not wish to have them. The all-union survey referred to above in fact provided some apparently new information about holdings of consumer durables and popular demand. Data for the most widespread or popular goods possessed by the workers in the sample are listed in table 2.10; the items have been arranged according to frequency of incidence.

The configuration of replies is largely self-explanatory, but a few points deserve comment. It would appear that there was still a significant undersupply of many common goods, especially those of domestic character. The low incidence of suites, or sets, of furniture may be connected with short-

Table 2.9   *Per Capita Consumption of Basic Cloths and Clothes as Percentage of "Rational Norms"*

	Per capita consumption (%)			"Rational norm," 1979
Items	1970	1980	1984	(square meters)
All cloths[a]	60.0	68.4	73.0	50.0
Cotton	67.9	76.2	81.7	31.2
Woolen	64.7	64.7	60.0	4.17
Silk	45.9	64.4	68.3	10.25
Linen	40.4	33.7	33.7	4.45
Articles of clothing				
Outer knitted garments, undergarments	39.5	48.5	49.2	13.41
Footware (leather, textile, and mixed)	82.6	88.2	85.4	3.63

SOURCES: Iu. A. Gusev, p. 53; *Narodnoe khozyaistvo SSSR v 1984*, p. 460.

[a] The cloth quantities presumably include an allowance for household linens, etc., along with personal garments.

Table 2.10   *Holdings of Consumer Durables and Desire to Obtain Them*

Article	Percentage having them	Percentage wanting them
Refrigerator	73.2	14.6
TV (black and white)	69.3	10.2
Washing machine	63.9	19.2
Radio, record player	57.9	16.8
Vacuum cleaner	40.6	20.0
Carpet	38.7	24.6
Suite (set) of furniture	24.2	25.7
Furs	19.9	29.3
China	18.7	21.0
Motorcycle	13.7	9.0
Fashionable clothes	13.3	20.5
TV, color	10.0	23.2
Hi-fi	9.1	11.0
Car	8.0	9.1
Library	6.4	23.9
Antique items	5.0	4.9
(Etc.)		

SOURCE: V. Kh. Bigulov, A. O. Kryshtanovskii, and A. S. Michurin, *S. I.*, 1984, no. 4: 91.

ages of living space. Surprisingly few people expressed a desire for a car, but a large number wanted a library; both responses, one suspects, were influenced by the constraints of Soviet reality. The public is not yet car-minded, and books, especially "complete works," are popularly regarded as a good way of preserving value. They can be acquired gradually, look well, and assume extra worth if the author goes out of print. The figures given for other social groups are a little too complex for inclusion here, but it would seem that the collective farmers both possessed less and had slightly weaker acquisitive urges. The intelligentsia had higher rates of possession and more desire to obtain consumer goods. The only listed exception were motorcycles!

An account of the evil consequences that occur when supply does not match demand, nicely categorized as "departures from the socialist principle of distribution," was recently provided by Mikhail N. Rutkevich, an ideological official renowned for his orthodoxy. So authoritative a source merits brief quotation.[10]

The first "departure," he stated, was the result of administrative decisions in the sphere of wages, and included "the payment of unjustified bonuses,

payment for mere appearance on the job, the so-called *vyvodilovka,* etc."
The second departure comprised "illegal acts at work and in other places,
including the service sector . . . including theft, bribery, 'speculation,' poach-
ing, receipt of other types of unearned income, unauthorized absences, and
so on." In other words, too much unearned money was going into circula-
tion. "However," he continued,

> an honestly earned ruble, and an unearned ruble stolen from society, are
> externally indistinguishable. The possession by even a small part of the
> public of "on-the-side" money promotes a lax attitude that does not fit
> the social function of money under socialism . . . Particular harm is
> done to society when all kinds of parasites use significant sums to ac-
> quire property, organize expensive banquets for tens and hundreds of
> guests to mark weddings, memorial services, etc., build houses and
> dachas, and purchase luxury goods for parasitic consumption . . . These
> phenomena . . . have a destructive influence not only on persons work-
> ing in trade and the services . . . but on all politically and morally un-
> stable members of society.

The trade network is not alone responsible for the deficits; breakdowns
in economic mechanisms have to be taken into account as well. Consumers
tend to blame the shops, however. Dissatisfaction is greater when customers
come upon frequent infringements of trading rules,

> the concealment of goods, difficulties in handing in glass bottles, rude-
> ness, open and covert blackmail. Despite repeated instructions and pro-
> hibitions, there are frequent instances of the enforced sale of deficit
> goods as part of an [otherwise unsellable] set, together with the imposi-
> tion of unneeded services. Thus to get replacement parts that are not in
> stock, the car-owner must apply to a servicing center, where the charge
> for the part may be sold at much above its nominal cost . . .
>   Forms of concealed blackmail, whose fruits go straight into the
> pocket of the trade employee, are no less well-known. They include
> short weight, wrong change, inflated prices, bribes for under-the-
> counter sales, etc., etc. It is not necessary to carry out special surveys of
> public opinion or a content analysis of readers' letters to establish grow-
> ing public dissatisfaction with the general state of trade.

Shortfalls in Housing

For reasons that are not entirely clear, the Soviet authorities are relatively
forthcoming about the housing stock. At least, overall figures have been
published in the national statistic handbooks for many years now. Under-

provision in this sphere can therefore be judged a little better than in others. By 1986 "general usable living space" was said to stand at 14.8 square meters per capita for all urban and rural housing stocks, which works out at about 9.6 square meters of actual living area, excluding kitchens, bathrooms, corridors, and cupboards.[11]

The impact of a vigorous building program has been weakened by the poor quality of existing stock, demolition, and widespread dilapidation. By the mid-1980s the amount of accommodation was still, by West European standards, grossly inadequate. Occupancy was well above one person per room; although the declared "sanitary minimum" of 9 square meters of basic living space had been reached, the so-called rational norm of 13 square meters was still (to judge from the planned rate of building) a couple of decades off. Since existing space was, of course, unevenly distributed, both geographically and among social groups, acute problems remained for a large percentage of households.

Occasional published comment gives some idea of the extent and social consequences of the continuing shortage:

1. The 1985 issue of the national statistical handbook mentioned that "over 80 percent" of the urban population lived in "separate" flats. This suggested that something approaching 20 percent of urban families shared accommodations, or occupied other unsatisfactory types of dwelling.[12]

2. The housing shortage in Novosibirsk (population c. 1,357,000) in 1981 was illustrated in terms of room occupancy in a recent study by O. E. Bessonova (table 2.11). It is noteworthy that Novosibirsk then

Table 2.11   Rooms per Family in Novosibirsk (circa 1985) (percentage distributions)

Number of rooms occupied	Family size				
	1 pers.	2 pers.	3 pers.	4 pers.	5 pers.
One room	5	41	16	7	2
Two rooms	4	22	42	23	8
Three rooms	3	4	13	46	30
Four rooms	1	2	9	21	61

SOURCE: O. E. Bessonova, *Izvestiia Sibirskogo otdeleniia AN, prikladnaia ekonomika i sotsiologiia*, 1985, no. 1: 57.

NOTE: The figures were re-established from a careful diagram, but there are discrepancies of up to 6 percent in the percentage totals as calculated. Some of these may be due to gaps in the original data or to lack of response. No details were provided on the source of this information.

had a rating of 13.2 square meters of general usable space per capita, which was fairly average for large Russian cities. The figures cited, however, left no doubt about the degree of discomfort for many: 65 percent of all one-room units were occupied by families of two to five persons. Of course, the density may have been slightly overstated by the inclusion of "dead souls" (absent relatives) in residence surveys.

3. Vladivostok (population c. 576,000) had a per capita rating of about 12.8 square meters in 1981 and was thus somewhat below the national norm at that time. In 1979–80 the local party committee and city soviet introduced a plan to use 45 percent of new housing capacity to rehouse persons living in huts (*baraki*), dilapidated houses, attics, and cellars. Although 90 percent of the hut dwellers were rehoused, the plan was not fulfilled, leaving an urban waiting list of 40,000 persons, presumed to represent families totaling 120,000 members, or over a fifth of the population. Part of the problem, however, was said to be due to double-listing of residents; the authors of the study claimed that the demand for extra accommodation could be reduced to 10 percent of existing stock if the lists were regularized.[13]

4. In the autumn of 1984 some six million people, mostly young and single, lived in hostels. Such accommodation is satisfactory only in specific circumstances, for example, when it is of adequate quality, or occupied only temporarily. The space norm in hostels was recently raised from 4.5 to 6.0 square meters a person, and the demand for hostel places (according to an article by A. E. Kotliar and M. I. Talalai) exceeded supply by a quarter. A survey of 118 workers' hostels in 28 towns reported by the authors revealed considerable dissatisfaction (table 2.12). Laundry and other services were a rarity, and the majority of hostels had no dining facilities. "Situations not infrequently occurred when, as at the Kamyshinsk Cotton Combine, every third respondent considered a buffet meal not to be without danger to health, owing to the poor quality of the food." Sixty percent of the hostels lacked adequate furniture. About 11 percent of the residents "created families" yearly, but a third said they could not get married because of their living conditions.[14]

One further comment may be in order regarding satisfaction with housing. A study of six enterprises reported by A. G. Simakov found that overall only 22 percent of the workers were fully satisfied, and 14.6 percent were partly satisfied.[15] Of those living two to a room, 25 percent were satisfied, while among those who had their own room the proportion was 63 percent. Strangely enough, of those who had more than one room to themselves, only

Table 2.12   *Causes of Hostel Dwellers' Dissatisfaction*
(percentage of responses)

Causes of dissatisfaction	All persons	Single persons	Small families
Too many persons in a room	35.1	29.2	44.0
Noise, conditions prevent rest	33.6	23.8	48.2
Uncomfortable, lack of furniture	30.7	40.0	16.9
Unsatisfactory sanitation, hygiene	29.6	28.5	31.4
Lack of living rooms	24.4	21.1	29.2
Shortcomings in catering	19.5	22.0	15.7
Unsatisfactory conditions for study and leisure	16.4	19.7	9.5

SOURCE: A. E. Kotlyar and M. I. Talalai, *EKO,* 1984, no. 10: 142.

50 percent were satisfied. Families in the last category, Simakov observed, evidently begin to apply a different scale of values. This state of affairs appears to be another instance of improved supply raising expectations.

Some Conclusions

As may be gathered from the foregoing pages, the evidence is overwhelming that by the early 1980s there was very extensive dissatisfaction in the USSR with important aspects of material well-being there. Indeed, widespread consumer dissatisfaction is undoubtedly one of the mainsprings of the Gorbachev leadership's current campaign for social and economic reform. The authorities are uneasy about the living conditions of the populace, as compared to those of peoples in advanced capitalist lands. They may also regard economic deprivation as a destabilizing force in the future.

The most cogent explanations for public dissatisfaction must lie simply in the observed failure of the economy to raise incomes and reduce prices, while at the same time providing adequate supplies of consumer goods—despite the flood of official promises. Other, more subtle factors are also pertinent, however. For example, in a forthright interview with a Soviet journalist, the sociologist Vladimir Aleksandrovich Iadov claimed that part of the trouble lay in the fact that the public, particularly young people, were given an overoptimistic picture of their employment prospects and told "fairy tales" about what awaited them in their working lives. Disappointment was inevitable when they left school and confronted the realities of daily life.[16]

Iadov went on to say that "people's conscious perception of their social well-being" evolved over time, being affected both by "changes in their well-being, and by the specific life paths of different generations." Translated into clearer language, this statement means that expectations would continue to rise as time went by, so that improvements in living standards, which were not guaranteed, anyway, need not bring a greater level of satisfaction. Thus, it would seem that in this sphere, too, Soviet experience cannot easily demonstrate the superiority of Soviet society over bourgeois society.

Another factor possibly contributing to popular dissatisfaction was low state prices, particularly for certain foodstuffs, that maintained expectations at an impossibly high level. Thus a group of Soviet sociologists, in the autumn of 1987, said that in areas where supplies were adequate the demand for meat and meat products was "linked to physiological need." (They mentioned Moscow, Leningrad, and the Baltic republics as examples, though anyone familiar with the queues in Soviet cities would be prompted to question their judgment.) At existing state prices, they claimed, popular per capita consumption could rise to 85–86 kilos a year, which could not be justified on medical grounds. The implication behind their article was that some kinds of popular demand were encouraged by state subsidies and could be usefully—or harmlessly—reduced if prices rose.[17]

The burden of shortages of money, goods, and services is not borne equally by all members of society. But the Protasenko study cited above showed fairly convincingly that even people in the middle-income brackets find they have difficulty in making ends meet, not to mention the increasing dissatisfaction as pay packets get smaller. This, too, is a situation familiar in capitalist lands.

Some of the results examined above have such negative implications that anyone cognizant of the impediments to social research in the Soviet Union might wonder why they were revealed at all. Most predated Gorbachev's advent to power and the policy of *glasnost'*. Possible reasons include the gradual strengthening of Soviet sociology, perceived as a tool for social engineering; the academic nature of some disclosures; and the existence of a lobby of influential officials who no doubt hoped cautious revelation would promote improvement. As outside observers, we can only welcome sound research that helps us to understand Soviet society better.

In conclusion, attention should be drawn to a matter of considerable political import, though we have not considered it as such in the foregoing discussion. Given the scarcity of serviceable information on the Soviet people's political views, attitudinal studies like those presented here may serve as a passable substitute. In other words, it is reasonable to believe that what people could not say about the CPSU, they could say about their wage packets. Beyond that, much of the research being done in the USSR at present, particularly in this sphere, will hopefully serve as a baseline for the analysis of change in the future, a standard for measuring the degree to which Soviet society is or is not ridding itself of some major social ills.

3 | Deprivation Among Soviet Families

Results from a Survey of Soviet Emigrés

Introduction

The decision of the Brezhnev leadership in the early 1970s to allow a certain amount of emigration evoked considerable interest in the "sovietological" fraternity. Clearly, despite all the pitfalls, the considered experiences of Soviet citizens who had lived in the confines of Soviet reality could in some ways make up for the silence of the statistical handbooks. Between 1971 and 1981 about a third of a million people were allowed to leave. They were mostly Jews, though there were also groups of Armenians and ethnic Germans. By the early 1980s, when the flow was more or less halted, several closely knit and accessible colonies had been established in Israel, the United States, and West Germany.

The problem of poverty in the USSR, or some aspects of it, could, it seemed to me, be usefully explored through the experiences of formerly poor emigrés. With this intention I began a search for respondents who would agree to fill in an appropriate questionnaire. The first interviews were conducted in the summer of 1982 and took the form of a pilot study of 25 families, living mostly in the United States. Systematic interviewing began in the United States in September 1982 and was extended to Israel in January 1983. The application of questionnaires was completed everywhere by the end of May 1984, when the sample comprised responses from 348 family heads and 442 working members of the same families. The interviewers, former Soviet citizens with experience in this work, were paid for locating families (which was done by personal acquaintance or through friends), conducting the interviews, and making additional enquiries. The respondents, however, participated voluntarily, without payment. Assurances of anonymity were given in every case, though interviewers were asked to keep careful note of families' names and addresses, should clarification of answers be needed. These arrangements worked fairly well.[1]

Most of the questions were formulated in accordance with my own understanding of Soviet reality, after due consultation with former and present Soviet citizens. My perusal of the results of the study is best prefaced by a short account of the sample itself.

The Nature of the Sample

All but fifteen of the 348 families interviewed left the Soviet Union between 1978 and 1983, so the picture they presented related to the late Brezhnev era. I decided to focus analysis as far as possible on small but full families, *family* being understood to mean a group of persons who were related or closely associated, and who shared the same residence, and a "full family" being taken to include two parents and at least one child. In fact, all families contained a mother, and in all but 25 cases the head of the household was a man; 342 had between three and five members (table 3.1). Six two-member families were included because they were of particular interest for other reasons. All families contained at least one working member, and 322 had at least one resident child. Pensioners and unemployed adults appeared only as members of a family unit. The average family size was 3.91, a figure that

Table 3.1   *Distribution of Families by Size and Composition*

Number of family members	Number of families
Two-member families	6
Three-member families: father, mother, one child (72)[a]	100
Four-member families: father, mother, two children (123) father, mother, grandmother, one child (26)	172
Five-member families: father, mother, grandmother, two children (42) father, mother, grandfather, grandmother, one child (9)	65
Six- to eight-member families	5
Total	348

[a] There are, of course, numerous combinations of members. The most frequent combinations are shown, with the number of family units in parentheses.

may be arithmetically dismembered as follows: husband, 0.928; wife, 1.00; grandfather, 0.089; grandmother, 0.322; other adults, 0.063; and children, 1.508. The sample is fairly homogeneous in terms of family size and membership.

Income (and the likelihood of poverty) tends to vary considerably by age group. The lowest age accepted for the head of family (or principal earner) was 30 years in the last normal year of residence in the USSR (or "PNG" to use the Russian initials), so as to exclude persons whose earnings were low owing to youth or professional immaturity (table 3.2). Thirty-five or even 40 years would have been a better threshold for this purpose, but the difficulty of finding families precluded it. The average age of the wives was lower than that of their spouses, but even so most of them were 30 or more years of age. The sample contained 31 grandfathers and 114 grandmothers, of whom 21 and 106, respectively, were over normal retirement age. Of the 480 minors, 184 were six or under, and therefore not old enough for schooling. All but one of the remainder were in full-time study, reflecting the effectiveness of educational coverage in urban areas, even among the less privileged folk.

Income is central to any definition of poverty, so the parameters set for the selection of respondents were particularly stringent in this respect. Families were sought with a per capita "official" income of up to 70 rubles a month; individual working members were generally expected to have a gross official wage or salary of not more than 150 rubles a month. "Secondary" or side earnings were not to amount to more than 25 rubles a month per capita.

The reasons for choosing these limits are as follows. Seventy rubles is a moderate estimate of the amount that had to be earned in the late 1970s in order to match the per capita minimum budget requirement of 66.6 rubles per month proposed by Soviet welfare economists for small urban families in the early 1970s (see discussion on pp. 114–117 of next chapter). I am prepared to admit that a fuller allowance for inflation, income tax, and other likely outgoings could have taken the figure several rubles higher, but for sampling purposes I had an obvious interest in keeping the threshold as low as possible. My wage limit of 150 rubles a month was set significantly lower than the officially published average for 1979, 163.3 rubles, but high enough to make the location of respondents practicable. The permitted ceiling for secondary earnings, on the other hand, had to be set low to exclude persons who may have enjoyed a relatively high standard of living through intense activity of this kind.

The distribution of sample families was satisfactory in these terms and is shown in tables 3.3 and 3.4. The median per capita income was 54.0 rubles, and 36.8 percent of the families fell below the 51.4 ruble minimum budget requirement proposed for the mid-1960s. In the late 1970s, such families

Table 3.2 *Distribution of Family Members by Age*

	0–6	7–17	18–25	26–29	30–39	40–49	50–59	60+	Totals
Husbands	—	—	—	12	182	84	42	3	323
Wives	—	—	9	63	175	75	26	—	348
Grandfathers	—	—	—	—	—	—	5	26	31
Grandmothers	—	—	—	—	—	33	81	—	114
Other adults[a]	—	45	5	3	1	3	8	—	65
First children	84	200	—	—	—	—	—	—	284
Second children	97	92	—	—	—	—	—	—	189
Other children	3	4	—	—	—	—	—	—	7

Total number of adults: 881   Total number of children: 480
[a]The 65 "other adults" included 46 grown children still living with their parents. Of these, 42 were still engaged in some form of schooling, while the remainder were either employed or retired.

undoubtedly experienced severe hardship. Secondary income is by no means easy to estimate, being unevenly distributed and often illegal in character, as we shall demonstrate below. Nevertheless, we concluded that official earnings were supplemented in this manner by about 14.8 rubles per employee over the whole sample. Taking this into account, total per capita income (net official income plus all unofficial earnings, divided by the number of family members) rises to a per capita median of 60.9 rubles. Only 17.5 percent of the families had a per capita income of 70 rubles a month or more.

A breakdown of employed householders by occupational category is shown in table 3.5. As may be seen, the seven-part scale devised for this task distinguishes between manual and nonmanual jobs at three levels, with an additional category for degree-holding (but low-paid!) specialists.[2] No responsible managerial staff, or persons employed in agriculture, the army, or the police were included in the sample. Pensioners who were fully retired, and a few individuals who reported no employment, were also omitted from this table.

It will be noted that 11.7 percent of the employed persons were in unskilled occupations, manual and service. The jobs most commonly held by men at this level were laborer (6) and packer (5); and by women, checker, sorter (10), store guardian, and the like (5). We did, in fact, expect this group to be small in number, since families with skills thought to be marketable in capitalist society tend to predominate among emigrants. Moreover, for historical reasons, Soviet Jews are not popularly associated with menial jobs.

Most respondents (69.3 percent) were semi- or highly skilled manual workers, and what we might term middle- or high-grade service personnel. As may be seen from the table, the great majority of manual workers at these levels consisted of men; women predominated among the nonmanual workers. By far the most common occupations for men were those of fitter (37) (in U.S. English: machinist; skilled metal worker), driver (26), lathe or other kinds of machine operator (24), mechanic (21), electrician (17), plasterer, painter, or repairer (15), and welder (7). The women were most often nurses (35), bookkeepers (34), secretaries, clerks, and other office staff (32), laboratory or technical assistants (24), cashiers, accounts and planning clerks (14), kindergarten attendants (14), hairdressers and the like (11). The unskilled female manual workers were mostly in garment production (13).

The remaining 19.1 percent of the respondents held jobs normally requiring a degree. About two-thirds of them were men; their most common professions were those of engineer (18), teacher (19), cultural worker of various kinds (13), and physician (5). The sample is occupationally somewhat heterogeneous, but since poverty embraces many socio-occupational groups, this is not entirely disadvantageous for purposes of analysis.

Table 3.3 *Distribution of Families by Net Official Per Capita Income (rubles, monthly)*

Income	Number of families	Percent
29 rubles or less	6	1.7
30–34.9	6	1.7
35–39.9	16	4.6
40–44.9	28	8.1
45–49.9	49	14.1
50–54.9	85	24.5
55–59.9	82	23.6
60–64.9	53	15.2
65–69.9	19	5.6
70 rubles or more	3	0.9

N = 348 families   Median: 54.0 rubles

NOTE: The monthly per capita income shown in this table is net of income tax, trade-union dues, and gifts at the workplace. We have retained ruble fractions, as produced by our calculations, though given the nature of the variables they imply an overly high degree of accuracy. Most of the estimates, as averaged out, are best thought of as being indicative to within one or two rubles.

Table 3.4 *Distribution of Families by Total Per Capita Income (rubles, monthly)*

Income	Number of families	Percent
44.9 rubles or less	17	4.9
45–49.9	15	4.3
50–54.9	42	12.1
55–59.9	75	21.6
60–64.9	86	24.7
65–69.9	52	14.9
70–74.9	37	10.6
75–79.9	13	3.7
80 rubles or more	11	3.2

N = 348 families   Median: 60.9 rubles

Table 3.5   *Distribution of Adults by Current Occupational Category*

Occupational category	Husbands	Wives	Grand-fathers	Grand-mothers	Totals	Percent
Unskilled manual workers	13	20	0	0	33	4.7
Unskilled service personnel	10	31	3	5	49	7.0
Semiskilled manual workers	57	29	4	8	98	14.1
Middle-grade service personnel	29	117	3	8	153	22.5
Highly skilled manual workers	118	20	2	1	141	20.3
High-grade service personnel	11	70	2	3	86	12.4
Specialists or similar	85	44	0	3	132	19.0
Totals	323	331	14	28	696	100.0

NOTE: Since so many members of the "other adults" group (table 3.2) were in transitional situations between study and employment, they are omitted from analysis here and in table 3.6.

The educational attainments of the adults are shown in table 3.6. The figures reflect both the considerable advances made by the USSR in this sphere and the occupational configuration of the sample. Noteworthy are the relatively high levels of attainment in the "second" generation; the divergent distribution of men and women (the latter being rather more likely to have completed general school, or a SSUZ, but less likely to have gone on to full-time higher education); and the gaps between the older and second generations.

The ethnic composition of the sample requires little comment. The majority of respondents (86.1 percent) were, of course, Jews, while of the remainder 9.8 percent were Russian, 1.2 percent Ukrainian, 1.5 percent White Russian, and 1.3 percent Baltic or of undeclared origin. The overwhelming predominance of Jews does not, in my opinion, significantly affect the sample perception of those aspects of Soviet reality at issue here. To judge from their responses, most (if not all) participants were thoroughly sovietized and had experienced no other kind of life. The few, rather specific

Table 3.6   *Distribution of Adults by Educational Attainment*
(percentages of total numbers)

	Husbands (N = 323)	Wives (N = 348)	Grand-fathers (N = 31)	Grand-mothers (N = 114)
General school, classes 1–8	16.7	12.9	74.2	66.7
General school, complete, full-time	22.6	34.2	0.0	15.8
complete, part-time	9.9	1.1	3.2	0.9
PTU	26.0	4.3	3.2	0.0
SSUZ, full-time	7.4	28.4	12.9	2.6
part-time	4.3	10.9	0.0	2.6
VUZ, full-time	11.1	6.0	3.2	5.3
part-time	1.2	1.4	0.0	0.0
No education, or none revealed	0.6	0.6	3.2	6.1

NOTE: PTU: Low-grade vocational school; SSUZ: secondary special educational institution; VUZ: higher educational institution.

instances in which ethnicity might limit the generality of our argument are commented upon as occasion demands.

As for geographical location, nearly all the families lived in European areas of the RSFSR, the Ukraine, White Russia, and Moldavia. Six families came from the Baltic republics, however, and two did not reveal their place of residence. Fifty-eight percent lived in cities of over half a million inhabitants, mainly the republican capitals; on the other hand, some 12 percent came from small or very small towns. Two Ukrainian towns, Chernovtsy and Beltsy, together provided no less than 53 families. The fact that so many should have come from two small towns reflected the respondents' preference for living near former neighbors when they were in emigration.

Problems of Adequacy and Interpretation

The degree to which the sample is representative of the "Soviet poor" is a matter of central importance to the interpretation of the responses. It is not, however, something that is easily assessed, for the diversity of socio-occupational groups that make up the "poor" in Soviet society is great. In the small urban family with one or more working members, on which our study concentrates, occupation is a key factor in determining the level of material well-being. In general, the poor are employed in those low-paying branches where one would expect to find them: light industry, the consumer and service sectors, health, education, and culture. Persons in unmechanized jobs are much more likely to be low-paid than those in mechanized occupations. Persons with little or no skill also tend to find themselves at the bottom of the wage hierarchy in most sectors of the economy. A list of unprestigious and poorly paid jobs, as assessed by our respondents, is given in table 3.24 below.

I would not claim that the occupational configuration of the respondents closely matched that of the urban groups most likely to be poor. The proportion of skilled workers, medium-grade service personnel, and specialists was too great. I would, however, argue that this discrepancy hardly affects the usefulness of the exercise. It did, at least, reach the middle and upper layers of the poor, and most of the sample families lived well below the stipulated poverty threshold. The most common categories of the urban poor were well represented, and families from the smaller and economically neglected towns were prominent among respondents. My main aim was to describe and assess the life-styles and attitudes of people who themselves experienced material hardship. The sample was adequate for this purpose.

The difficulties of obtaining accurate facts from emigrés about their lives in the USSR are well known and require no more than a brief mention here. Information may be distorted principally by (*a*) the prevalence of negative attitudes to Soviet power; (*b*) a biased perception of Soviet reality; (*c*) a tendency to exaggerate former difficulties, to "open people's eyes" in the West; (*d*) conversely, a tendency to conceal difficulties or experiences considered shameful; (*e*) the invention of answers that, given the problems of access to the USSR, cannot be verified; (*f*) loss of detail due to memory failure; (*g*) error, technical carelessness, or intervention on the part of interviewers.

While not denying the relevance of these difficulties, I have good reason to believe that they have not greatly affected the information assembled here. First, the questionnaire was concerned almost entirely with matters of daily life and contained little of political or emotional import. Second, the responses to a number of questions suggested that few respondents suffered political or ethnic discrimination sufficient to bias their judgment on mundane matters. Distortion would arguably be less likely in the presence of interviewers who were themselves brought up in the Soviet Union and thought to have a balanced assessment of it. My own perusal of the survey results produced several reassuring instances of identity between respondents' information and fact deducible from other sources.

As for the problems of recollection, much of the detail requested was very familiar to the respondents, and likely to be recalled with reasonable accuracy. The time lag between the year described and interviewing was not great. Finally, I have good reason to trust the efforts of the interviewers. All were anxious to maintain opportunities for further employment; most would gladly have done more interviewing, had bona fide families been available. No discrepancies suggesting carelessness or malpractice came to light.

All social surveys, no matter how carefully conducted or checked, tend to throw up puzzling or erratic responses, and the 790 interviews in our data banks (348 plus 442) are no exception. The most troublesome instances were traced and corrected, but this still left a small residue I could well have done without. They included, apart from unwanted silences, a few cases of clearly untypical consumption; unusual expenditures or possessions; a wide range of personal estimates; a few obviously absurd opinions; and (despite all efforts at eradication) some apparently erroneous replies. The difficulty and cost of interviewing families that fitted my parameters precluded the exclusion of whole cases on account of an occasional blemish.

The problem has been dealt with in the most commonly accepted ways. Sometimes the wayward cases were statistically insignificant, or fitted into the end categories of frequency distributions, where they did little harm. When this did not happen our practice has been to exclude, with due note, a few percentage points at each end of the distribution of responses, so that the pattern produced by the overwhelming majority of participants might be presented in a less encumbered manner. Given the nature of sociological analysis, and the circumstances of the study, I consider this to be by and large tolerable. Each response made up only 0.287 percent of all responses in the "family" data bank and 0.226 percent of those in the "working members" data bank. A handful of questions was added to the questionnaire after systematic interviewing had been going on for some months, and when this occurred the reduced number of respondents to whom they were addressed is indicated.

I am satisfied that the problems of data collection, though palpable, were not serious enough to affect the general reliability of the conclusions set out in these pages.

Low Pay and Common Reactions

In this section I shall consider the nature of earnings among the families in the sample, and the more common reactions to low pay. It is convenient for present purposes to distinguish two broad categories of earnings, namely, legal, "official" pay at the regular place, or places, of employment and what may be called secondary, "unofficial" earnings, both legal and illegal, in money or kind, at work or outside it.

Official earnings are paid monthly (sometimes with a fortnightly advance) as wages or salaries. In some cases the sums are fixed, and known precisely in advance; in others they vary somewhat according to time input, goods produced, or bonuses, and so on. Where such variation occurred, our respondents were asked to enter an average figure. The distribution of gross official pay for working husbands and wives separately is shown in table 3.7. The average for husbands was 117.1 and for wives 83.3 rubles a month, while the weighted average for both was 99.9 rubles. This kind of sex differential is related to the lower average age of the wives, to occupational and educational differences, and the sad female monopoly of the child-bearing function (see also pp. 101–106 below). But in the case of poor families the discrepancy may well be increased by other factors, for instance, by poor husbands' having less chance than rich ones of helping their wives into better-paid positions. The sociology of this matter merits further investigation.[3]

Poor people should not, according to common wisdom, suffer significant

Table 3.7 *Official Earnings of Husbands and Wives, with Reported Deductions*

Wage group (rubles, monthly)[a]	Men	Women	Reported deductions (average, rubles)[b]	Reported deductions (average, percent)
1–79.9	5	94	4.7	6.7
80–89.9	15	84	6.4	7.7
90–99.9	32	81	7.4	7.7
100–109.9	20	40	9.8	9.6
110–119.9	37	19	11.5	10.1
120–129.9	51	9	11.6	9.6
130–139.9	45	3	13.1	10.0
140–149.9	42	1	14.2	10.1
150–159.9	47	0	16.3	10.9
160 and over	29	0	18.7	11.2

Men: N = 323   Women: N = 331

[a]Within each wage group the differential varied by a maximum of 1.3 rubles between the sexes (the maximum divergence occurring in the 100–109.9 ruble group).

[b]The reported deductions deviated from official rates, calculated at the category midpoints, by an average of only 66 kopecks.

loss of income through deductions at the source. The most important deduction from the Soviet wage packet takes the form of income tax, to which must be added the small but now almost universal union dues. The extent to which poor people are so burdened may be judged from the table. Not only were the deductions in most cases quite sizable, but they were also rather insensitively imposed. Thus respondents in the lowest wage groups were paying little less, in percentage of income, than those in the highest. (In addition, about a third of the sample also reported unavoidable gifts to workmates and colleagues, averaging two to three rubles a month, but such gifts may have been reciprocated in some cases and are not reflected in these figures.)

The attitudes of low earners to their modest pay is of prime interest in any sociological analysis. Of the 442 respondents who supplied such information, some 24.0 percent thought that they were "very badly," and 35.9 percent "badly," paid. However, 38.9 percent rated their pay as tolerable, and 0.9 percent thought it was "good." We found no clear relationship between pay and satisfaction levels, which suggests that other factors were responsible for the latter. When asked what sum would be required to provide a minimal satisfactory standard of living for their families, the same respondents entered figures averaging no less than 51 percent above their income. It is not surprising that 27.5 percent stated they were "always" short of money before receiving their pay packet, and 44.6 percent said it happened "frequently." Only 4.8 percent rarely, or never, encountered such difficulty. Six percent of the respondents admitted to having some cash in hand, but 36.8 percent possessed savings accounts. The average deposit was 291 rubles, or just over a quarter of the national per capita figure.[4]

One consequence of continuing financial difficulty was a vast amount of pre-payday borrowing. Over 80 percent of the respondents said that they did this, on average, eight times a year. Nearly all of the borrowing was in the 10–30 ruble range, over a period of three to ten days. The creditors were, in roughly equal measure, relatives, friends, neighbors, and colleagues. I would hesitate to suggest a magnitude for these activities throughout the economy, but the sums involved must, in the aggregate, have been vast.

Secondary Income

The low-paid worker might be expected to ease his lot by earning more money, through state-approved channels or outside them. Such extra, or secondary, income may be derived from: (*a*) overtime, or employment in second jobs; (*b*) illegal activities at the workplace; or (*c*) private work, legal or illegal, outside the workplace, during the individual's own time. Let us now look at these sources in a little more detail.

To judge from official data, overtime at the place of employment has not in recent years been widespread in the Soviet economy, at least outside agriculture. Managements are said to be reluctant to pay the high overtime rates, and hidden labor reserves may make it unnecessary, except at times of crisis. Our returns for the 442 working respondents showed that although nearly half had endeavored to find extra sources of legal income at their workplace, only 65, or 14.7 percent, worked overtime. Earnings from it varied in most cases between 10 and 30 rubles a month, with a median figure of 20.4 rubles. Such work was curiously distributed, insofar as it was intensive, averaging three to twelve hours a week in almost 80 percent of the cases; however, only about 15 percent of the practitioners recognized it as overtime, as such, or received payment for it. The Soviet state must benefit greatly at a national level from this omission. Second jobs, I found, were rather uncommon, as only 22 respondents took them up. They required on average six hours a week and brought in around 20 rubles a month. When averaged across all working respondents, overtime and second jobs were responsible for around 3.5 rubles of monthly earnings and did not greatly ease financial pressures.

Of those who took on extra work, the majority (84.9 percent) did so primarily to earn extra money. Each respondent was invited to enter other reasons in order of importance, and an interesting pattern emerged: 77.1 percent did so at the insistence of the management; 57.7 percent because it was socially accepted; 48.6 percent did so to help workmates; 22.9 percent said they worked extra time because they found it interesting; and 12.5 percent because it improved their chances of promotion. Two other frequently mentioned reasons are, in my opinion, worthy of note. No less than 36.2 percent of the extra-timers said they worked "for the good of society," which suggests a fair degree of social commitment; on the other hand, 33.3 percent said they did extra work because of "the insistence of party organs," which provides some indication of political pressure at this point.

The reasons most commonly given for *not* doing extra work, despite financial pressures, were a heavy working week (83.3 percent); the impossibility of finding such work (78 percent); lack of time (73.3 percent); and domestic obligations (66.4 percent). As for attitudes toward illegal earnings, 12.8 percent of the respondents considered that it was "very important" to avoid them, and another 29.7 percent said it was "important" for them to do so, leaving a residue of 41.9 percent who were prepared to sin, should the opportunity present itself. Low pay may, of course, encourage mobility, and indeed some 33.7 percent of the sample said they had indeed sought new, higher-paid jobs.

The sample also produced interesting evidence of illegal money-making at the workplace. In fact, 124 people, or 19.0 percent of all employed

Table 3.8   *Illegal Earnings at the Workplace*

	Use of facilities for personal gain			Bribes			Sale (theft) of goods or services		
	Number	%[a]	Amt.[b]	Number	%[a]	Amt.[b]	Number	%[a]	Amt.[b]
Men	62	19.2	27.5	8	2.5	29.5	17	5.3	27.0
Women	16	4.8	19.2	9	2.7	20.0	12	3.6	24.1

Men: N = 87   Women: N = 37.
[a] Percentage of all employed persons.
[b] Average amount obtained, in rubles per month.

spouses (26.9 percent of the husbands and 11.2 percent of the wives), were involved. As may be seen from table 3.8, by far the most common form was the abuse of work facilities and materials; there were fewer admissions of bribery or the sale of illegally procured goods or services. No one entered more than one type of involvement. It may be that such activities, being somewhat shameful, were understated; the questionnaire, to avoid possible embarrassment, did not seek more detail. The configuration of other replies would not, however, suggest extensive concealment. The sharp differentiation between men and women in the degree of abuse is noteworthy, but may have had as much to do with differences of opportunity as with criminal propensity. The effect of these activities on the family purse was remarkably even, the monthly "take" averaging 27.6 rubles for men, 21.0 rubles for women, which gives an average of 4.9 rubles for all working spouses.

As for gainful activities outside the workplace, 160 respondents, or 36.2 percent of those to whom this part of the questionnaire was applied, reported earnings from such sources. Men were again much more likely to engage in them than women (45.6 as against 17.1 percent). There were only five reports of more than one activity of this type being carried on by a single person, but 69 individuals combined it with illegal practice at the workplace. None of the respondents entered money-making activities that would per se have been actionable under Soviet criminal law. But all private earnings are subject to relatively high rates of income tax, and those not revealed for this purpose are in effect illegal. In practice, people declare such earnings only if they are a sole or obvious source of income, or if it is hard to conceal them (the two characteristics normally being interdependent). Thus, most of the activity registered by the sample was in fact outside the law. Of the six respondents who let living space (a relatively overt form of private enterprise), only one declared it for tax purposes; of 53 who engaged in some form of private practice or gave lessons, only four reported it as being legally registered.

The range of outside activities, their periodicity, and the earnings yielded by them are summarized in table 3.9. The pattern is rather uneven, but the main features contain few surprises. The most common work took the form of repairs, as one might expect from the skilled people who formed the bulk of the sample. The fact that so few people were involved in cleaning and childminding presumably follows from the shortages of living space, reasonable access to day nurseries, and the presence of so many grandmothers. Many people, particularly those engaged in "private practice," showed a curious reluctance to specify what they did. Some of this work may be safely inferred from the respondents' occupational profiles, and I have included such cases at the foot of the table. Other individuals may have undertaken menial tasks that they preferred not to disclose.

I was not able to perceive any significant correlation between engagement in illegal gainful activity and the individual's level of education. The listing itself shows that the variety of skills offered extended across the occupational spectrum. The sporadic nature of the work and variations among cases complicated estimation of the sums earned (more so, I believe, than in the case of illegal activities at a regular place of work), but the median gain

Table 3.9 *Private Activities Outside the Workplace*

	Cases reported		Months per annum	Hours weekly	Average monthly income[a]
	Number	Percent			
Repair Work	78	47.3	8	9	18
Selling	7	4.2	6	5	11
Lessons	5	3.0	6	13	13
Artwork	5	3.0	6	15	25
Cleaning	4	2.4	6	10	13
Childminding	3	1.8	10	10	10
Garden work	1	0.6	2	60	3
Home products	2	1.2	8	10	13
Private practice[b]	48	29.1	10	11	23
Other activities[c]	12	7.3	6	12	13

N = 165 cases of employment, shared among 160 respondents.

[a] Months averaged and recalculated over a year. All income figures are to the nearest ruble.

[b] Including service by: medical personnel (6), hairdressers (5), drivers (4), and electricians (4).

[c] Including six cases of renting living space.

Table 3.10   *Motivation for Private Work (Percent)*

	Very important	Important	Not important
Need of money	93	7	0
Good income as compared with main job	28	55	17
Need of products so obtained	8	23	69
Access to people or services	10	48	42
Usefulness to society	1	37	62
Insistence of family, friends	2	27	71
Personal interest	1	28	71
Other	1	24	75

NOTE: All statistics relating to opinions here and below are given to the nearest full percentage point.

was 26.7 rubles for each month of involvement. This in turn averaged out at 10.0 rubles a month on an annual basis for all 442 respondents.

The main motive for participating in outside activities was financial, as was the case with overtime. All practitioners described financial need as "very important," or "important," while 83 percent thought such activities were profitable as compared with their main job (table 3.10). Human nature being what it is, however, several nonfinancial motives (access to people or services, social usefulness, insistence of friends, and interest) were also quoted.

Two problems require comment by way of conclusion to this section. The first is the overall impact of secondary earnings on poor people's income. Though overtime and the like may be recalled with a fair degree of accuracy, illegal earnings at the workplace, and especially earnings outside it, are more difficult to quantify. Averaging all such earnings across the whole sample is a risky business, no matter how it is done. But with this proviso we would estimate that such activities raised family income in all by 28.7 rubles, or 7.3 rubles per capita, monthly. This is 12.1 percent of total per capita income (table 3.4).

Second, there is the problem of typicality of these earnings across other social groups. It will be noted that in all, 215 persons of the 442, or 48.6 percent, indulged in illegal gainful activity of one kind or another.[5] Families with very large secondary incomes were specifically excluded from the sample, although such families doubtless exist. Our interviewers could freely include families with secondary earnings of up to 25 rubles a month per capita, and there was no difficulty in locating them. If the incidence of such cases were very different in the population at large, we feel that this would have been reflected in the sample results (though admittedly, Jewish families may have shown more personal initiative in this respect). In this case, it would seem that participation in the "second economy" is a powerful factor in raising living standards among the Soviet poor.

Pensioners' Income

Pension rates in the Soviet Union are fairly generous in relation to earnings, but in absolute terms the sums paid are modest. Most types of pension are also service-related, so an incomplete work record may result in a partial pension or even ineligibility. Soviet social security (like most other national systems) is intricate and cannot be discussed within the framework of this report.

The Soviet authorities are happy to publicize the existence of the system and publish data on aggregate pension payments. At the same time there is a marked reluctance to provide proper figures on the distribution of payments among recipients, no doubt because the lower rates entail considerable hardship. The amounts received as pension by 127 grandparents in the sample families are thus of some interest (table 3.11). The level of payments was indeed low. Eighteen grandmothers declared no income at all, and no less than 35 of the grandparents did not achieve the existing "full" state minimum of 45 rubles, their pensions being "partial" owing to an inadequate employment record. The average pension among recipients who received more than the minimum was only 56.9 rubles. In addition, seven people received disablement pensions averaging 48.5 rubles.[6]

Table 3.11   *Old-Age Pensions Among Grandparents*

Rubles	Number of persons	Percent
0–19.9	1	0.8
20–29.9	8	6.3
30–39.9	12	9.4
40–44.9	14	11.0
45–49.9	26	20.4
50–59.9	21	16.5
60–69.9	19	15.0
70–79.9	6	4.7
80 and over	2	1.6
No income declared	18	14.2

NOTE: A few grandparents retained full-time jobs, though over retirement age.

We have no reason to believe that such modest sums were untypical among old people in poor families. Low pay translates into lower pension rates, and a reduced or interrupted service record is especially common among elderly women who moved from village to town, or who had to stay at home and look after children. Ironically, in families already experiencing material hardship, the older generation has less chance to be self-supporting.

The Question of Unemployment

In capitalist lands unemployment is, of course, closely related to poverty. Given official denials of the existence of unemployment in the USSR before *perestroika* began, the question of how far the people in the sample were subject to it is of special interest. *Unemployment* was defined for this purpose as the lack of a main job for over a month, despite active efforts to find work more or less commensurate with given skills or ability, in the same, or another, acceptable district.

All the husbands and (no less significantly) 95.2 percent of the wives in our sample were in full-time employment. Our 442 working respondents entered a mere eighteen instances of unemployment throughout their careers, of which only eleven had occurred within ten years previous to the year described. A few people became unemployed for genuine or assumed failure of health, since sickness benefits were successfully applied for in eleven cases. Nine instances of unemployment were voluntary, prompted by low pay, unsatisfactory working conditions, or differences with the management. One person lost a job through enterprise closure, and five for political reasons or because of anti-Semitic prejudices. I take this, incidentally, as another demonstration of the generally apolitical stance of our respondents in their daily lives.

These few facts leave no doubt that people of the kind represented in our sample were little troubled by the specter of unemployment. Perhaps, as a consequence of their financial vulnerability, they avoided it more carefully than others. It may well be that Soviet urban poverty was at that time rarely caused or worsened by unemployment, and so in this respect differs markedly from urban poverty in advanced capitalist societies.

Living Conditions

The great majority of sample families lived in single- or multiple-occupancy flats owned by local councils or individual enterprises (table 3.12). Such flats

Table 3.12   *Distribution of Families by*
Type of Dwelling and Living Space

Type of dwelling	Families		Average per capita living space	Persons per room
	Number	Percent		
Flats				
1. Single-occupancy council flat	211	60.6	8.3	1.9
2. Single-occupancy enterprise/organization flat	11	3.2	8.1	1.9
3. Cooperative flat	8	2.3	9.0	2.0
Houses				
4. Separate house with amenities	5	1.4	9.6	1.9
5. Separate house without amenities	31	8.9	8.5	1.9
Rooms (Multiple Occupancy)				
6. Room(s) in a communal flat	66	19.0	6.2	2.7
7. Room(s) rented privately	7	2.0	6.4	3.0
8. Hostel	5	1.4	5.3	3.3
Other	4	1.1	4.4	2.5

N = 348 families

were by far the most common type of housing in Soviet towns in the late 1970s. Of the other dwellings represented, the most prestigious, and possibly best appointed, were private (that is, cooperatively owned) flats and houses with modern amenities. The houses without amenities varied in quality and were most often located in suburbs or in smaller provincial towns. The least fortunate families still occupied privately rented rooms and hostels. My first generalizations will cover single-occupancy, publicly owned flats (types 1 and 2 in the table) and the living conditions associated with them.

Single-Occupancy Flats

Let us begin with the amount of living space. As may be seen from table 13.12, the average was a little over 8 square meters per person, which was apparently close to the national figure.[7] This suggests that even if poor people have worse housing conditions than others, there is no simple correlation between poverty and floor area. At the same time none of the 222 families housed in these flats had more than three rooms at its disposal, and average occupancy was 1.9 persons per room, a very high rate by Western standards. Overcrowding was common in the localities represented: 88.1 percent of the respondents reported that their local authorities would accept applications for rehousing only from persons with less than five square meters. Overcrowding to this degree would be likely to qualify as living in "slum" conditions in advanced capitalist societies; but this term, like *poverty,* could not at that time be used to describe Soviet housing in published sources.

The most usual space allocated on rehousing was 7–9 square meters, although a few authorities granted 12–13 meters. The pattern of response to such a situation provides another example of how popular attitudes may be molded by daily realities, without regard to standards in other societies. No less than 40.3 percent of the respondents considered that they did, in fact, have enough space; 34.6 percent thought the space at their disposal was rather inadequate; and only 24.6 percent found it grossly inadequate. Dissatisfaction was naturally highest in the most crowded households.

With regard to household amenities, some were available as frequently as in advanced capitalist countries. All families had electricity; nearly all had running water and some form of gas; and 95.9 percent had the benefit of a lavatory that worked (table 3.13). Baths, central heating, and the availability of hot water were less satisfactory. Given that we are dealing with low-income families, the incidence of telephones was very high. This may have been due to shared usage and the low cost of calls.

The overall capital and decorative state of the housing was said, in 80–90 percent of the cases, to be fair or tolerable. Only a tiny minority of respondents—one percent or less—reported them to be very good. Heating, however, was a problem for 13.6 percent of the families, and damp troubled 14.9 percent. As for unwanted animal life, 25.7 percent recorded the presence of insects, and 13.5 percent that of mice; but there were no reports of rats.

Soviet authorities make much of the claim that public housing costs in the USSR are nominal, amounting to only a few kopecks per square meter.[8] It is interesting, in view of this, to consider the outgoings reported by families occupying publicly owned flats. Since the accommodations varied in size and location, and rent sometimes included heating and hot water, the range of payment was great. I found it expedient to assess per capita outgoings as rent plus the cost of other services, but minus the cost of repairs (of which more in a moment). Using this definition, we find that nearly all the families

Table 3.13   *Domestic Amenities in Publicly
Owned, Single-Occupancy Flats*

| Amenity | Families | | Percent in working order |
	Number	Percent	
Running water	222	100.0	97.7
Lavatory	222	100.0	95.9
Electricity	222	100.0	100.0
Gas	221	99.5	99.5
Bathroom	188	86.7	83.3
Central heating	189	85.1	84.6
Hot water	152	69.1	68.2
Telephone	121	56.8	56.3

living in council- and enterprise-owned flats reported per capita payments of between 2.0 and 12.5 rubles per month, with a mean of 5.1 rubles, or 9.4 percent of their official per capita income. This is much greater than the figure of 2.7 percent listed in the workers' and employees' average family budget published in the 1979 statistical handbook.[9]

Repairs were evidently a problem, in that so many devolved on the tenants themselves. Although, over a five-year period, only 1 percent of the families did any structural work, between 90 and 95 percent carried out repair of household amenities and the decoration of common passages. Table 3.14 shows how much of this work was done by the occupants themselves and how much by privately hired workmen. Irregular outgoings of this nature are particularly difficult to estimate retrospectively, but the great majority of respondents (some 80 percent) entered figures ranging from 10–60 rubles a year.

An all-too-familiar problem for public housing authorities in the West is nonpayment of rent and service charges. As far as we are aware, no information of this kind is published in the USSR. The sample returns indicated that during the last four years of normal residence, only nine families or their close relatives fell into arrears with their rent, on a total of 23 occasions. This resulted in warnings and in two fines, of two and four rubles. The rate of failure to pay electricity, gas, and telephone bills was even lower. The reasons for such exemplary fulfillment of obligations lie, no doubt, in the small sums involved and in the comprehensive system of housing offices that can put pressure on tenants. There were no cases of eviction.[10]

As for housing in general, over 90 percent of all respondents thought that

Table 3.14   *Responsibility for Repair Work
in Publicly Owned Flats (percent)*

Type of repair	Housing office	Privately hired labor	Tenants them-selves	No repair over 5 years
Structural repair	19.2	0.5	0.5	79.9
Repair of domestic amenities	56.4	19.5	19.1	5.0
Decoration of common parts	23.7	35.6	30.1	10.5

N = 219

the more opulent people in Soviet society were better, or much better, accommodated than the poor (in other words, that housing conditions were indeed socially differentiated). The main reasons for disadvantage were held to be lack of money for improvement (86.6 percent of responses); lack of the influence needed for betterment (84.2 percent); lack of money to buy a cooperative flat (62.3 percent); and too many dependents (40.8 percent). Conversely, only 4 percent thought that poor people were without a desire to improve their living conditions.

The scope of the survey did not allow me to investigate changes in respondents' living conditions over time, but I found that 32.5 percent of them had lived in buildings less than ten years old. Thus, despite continued overcrowding, many had gained from the long-term improvements in Soviet housing.

Multiple-Occupancy (Communal) Flats

The Soviet "communal" flat (type 6 in table 3.12) imposes its own constraints on peoples' lives, as was revealed by the responses of the 66 sample families so accommodated. These families were divided almost equally between those occupying one and those occupying two rooms. The flats housed on average 3.3 families, or between six and twelve persons. Living space in them averaged only 6.2 square meters per capita, so it is hardly surprising that of the 59 families who provided an overall assessment, 17 said their living space was inadequate, and 42 said it was grossly inadequate. One of the few advantages of the communal flat would appear to be its lower rent, which averaged 3.7 rubles per capita for all the "communal" occupants in the sample. Yet at 6.9 percent of official income, it was still above the average cited in the 1979 handbook.

People living in communal flats must, of course, share kitchen, bathroom, and corridor. All, or nearly all, of the flats occupied by sample families had running water, sanitation, electricity, gas, and central heating. But other amenities were more problematic. Thirty-one flats were without a supply of hot water, and four had hot-water systems that did not work; bathing facilities were absent in sixteen cases and not usable in another nine. Just over a half of the flats had telephones. Vermin were much more of a problem than in single-occupancy flats, as there were 45 reports of insects, 32 of mice, and 6 of rats. A much higher proportion of tenants reported structural and maintenance problems.[11] At the same time, there was hardly less involvement in repair and decoration work: 42 families declared they normally did, or paid for, domestic repairs, and 28 took responsibility for decoration of the corridors. The most typical outgoings for repair and decoration averaged 32 rubles a year.

Difficulty in making payments also seemed rather more common among dwellers in communal flats, with (over the same four years) 21 cases of arrears with rent, 6 cases with electricity, and 8 with gas. None of these, however, entailed fines of more than two or three rubles.

Despite their drawbacks, the communal flats covered by our survey were not the exclusive preserve of poor people; incomes as high as 150 rubles were reported among neighbors. As for the residents' occupational configuration, the trades and professions named were rather evenly spread over the categories we have used for analysis here, with an admixture of pensioners. In fact, specialists were most heavily represented (24.3 percent) and managerial staff least represented (3 percent). In the overwhelming majority of the cases, social relations were characterized as "good" or "average." According to the Soviet economist G. S. Sarkisian, by 1980 no less than a fifth of all urban families were still in communal accommodation.[12] It is reasonable to suppose that conditions in most such flats approximated to those occupied by the families in our sample.

Cooperative Flats

The presence in the poverty sample of eight families with "cooperative" or private flats requires comment. Not only are such flats difficult to come by, but purchasers are normally required to deposit one-third of the cost before occupancy, and the monthly repayments on the remainder, even at nominal rates of interest, may be considerable. A poor family is most likely to acquire a cooperative flat if (*a*) it had an opportunity to buy at an earlier, lower price (because owners could legally resell only at the original purchase price)[13]; (*b*) it receives a propitious offer of help from relatives or friends; or (*c*) it is in desperate need of living space, and prepared to take on a relatively heavy financial burden.

In four of the eight cases in our sample, rent, without repair costs, absorbed around 13 percent of family income. All of the eight flats were located in large towns; six were occupied by families of skilled workers and middle-grade white-collar personnel, having an average total per capita income of 62 rubles. The two cheapest flats (costing, untypically, 5 and 12 rubles a month, without repairs) were occupied by householders with low-level skills who may have had caretaker responsibilities. Floor space in this sector ranged from 5.3 to 15.0 square meters per capita, with an average of 2.2 dwelling rooms per family, an apportionment by no means generous.

Other Types of Housing

Other families in the sample lived in houses without modern amenities (31); privately rented rooms (7); and hostels (5).[14] Our analysis so far has not revealed any social characteristics by which these, probably the worst-housed people in the sample, could be distinguished. Their dwellings, however, fitted well-known stereotypes.

The houses were rather small, averaging 2.4 rooms, and provided living space at the rate of 8.5 square meters per capita. The lack of modern conveniences was in many cases serious. Although all had electricity and 28 had gas, 6 had no running water, 17 were without sanitation, and none had hot water, a bath, or central heating. There was only one telephone among them. Twenty-two of the families in question reported damp; in the three groups named above, 18, 23, and one family, respectively, reported insects, mice, and rats. Dwellings of this type were more costly to run because of their heating requirements and repairs. The basic monthly outgoings for housing tax, services, and heating averaged 18.3 rubles, or 4.8 rubles per capita a month. Nearly all repairs, regardless of type, were done by the owners, or at their own expense, and cost an average of 14 rubles a month.

Private renting is usually regarded as an undesirable option in the USSR, mainly because of its high cost, inconvenience, and at times dubious legality. The limited size of the questionnaire did not allow extra investigation of the few families thus lodged, but since so little is known about the practice, the points that emerged deserve mention. The amounts of space rented were minimal, averaging 6.4 square meters per head, with an occupancy of 3.0 persons per room. Family rents averaged 42.3 rubles, or 12.4 rubles per capita monthly. Private renting is usually done on a fairly short-term basis, unless circumstances dictate otherwise. Yet five of the families had occupied their privately rented quarters for up to three years. Five considered the space at their disposal to be inadequate, or grossly inadequate. Five families were without hot water or a bath, and four had no central heating.

Among the five families living in hostels, per capita allotments of space fell to 5.3 square meters, and very high figures were given for the use of some communal amenities. Two hostels were evidently without proper sanitation; families complained of inadequate heating, dampness, and the presence of vermin. Three of the families had lived in these conditions for five years or more. One advantage of such accommodation is popularly held to be its low cost; but it is noteworthy that the families in our sample paid 3.8 rubles per capita monthly—by no means a nominal sum for low earners.

Variation by District

How far the urban poor conglomerate in their "own" districts is another matter that, given the silence of Soviet scholarship, calls for attention. The obvious occurrence in their home towns (particularly Odessa, Kiev, and Leningrad) of such differentiation was affirmed by 11.2 percent of the sample, while another 57.2 percent said that it was to some extent discernible. The remainder said there was none, or could not comment.

Such hesitation is, of course, understandable. In capitalist countries, differentiating tendencies are strong. Local communities may be vociferous and have more influence over their environment than their Soviet counterparts; a good deal of property is privately owned; and although council controls are real enough, the quality of commercial services will tend to vary with local needs. Conglomerations of the poor may be encouraged by the reluctance of richer or more influential people to live in unattractive or polluted areas. In the Soviet Union, by contrast, far-reaching standardization of urban development, a constant housing shortage, nominal rents, and the absence of private commerce have tended to mask, rather than reflect, social distinctions.

The respondents who distinguished poor districts in their own towns had rather diverse views on what characterized them. The features judged to be unsatisfactory were, in descending order of frequency: housing (65.9 percent of the responses); communal services (61.0 percent); physical safety (51.0 percent); shopping facilities (45.1 percent); the condition of the streets (39.0 percent); transport (31.3 percent); and the quality of the air (23.6 percent). Some 60 percent of the respondents located the poor district they had in mind within two kilometers of dirty or unhealthy production enterprises. Respondents were asked to say when they thought construction of the given district had started. Of the 205 who replied, 37 percent entered 1960 to 1980. This suggests that local authorities have been unable to upgrade standards merely by new building. In other words, poor districts are not necessarily old districts, and they continue to form as the years go by.

As for apartment houses, most respondents considered them to be socially mixed, regardless of location. The Soviet elite (defined at this point as specialists and highly paid personnel) were nevertheless thought likely to en-joy more exclusive housing. Thus 50.4 percent of the respondents were of the opinion that specialists predominated in houses belonging to large min-istries and organizations; 28.9 percent thought that this was also true of cooperative apartment houses; and only four respondents (0.9 percent) thought specialists would be numerous in apartment houses belonging to local soviets.

Furniture and Household Durables

Soviet society has long since reached the stage at which the average family seeks to equip its home with the accoutrements of modern living: comfort-able furniture, appropriate decoration, and household gadgetry. Finding the necessary articles in the shops is still difficult, however; confined living space gives little scope for embellishment; and poverty inevitably places its own limitations on purchases. Since no comprehensive study of poor people's fur-niture, or of what Soviet statisticians term "cultural, domestic, and house-hold goods" (electrical equipment, kitchen and other gadgetry), had ever, to my knowledge, been published, brief sections on these topics were included in the questionnaire.

As for furniture, virtually all families owned tables, chairs, beds, and wardrobes in apparently adequate quantities. Most pieces of such furniture, however, were rather old and had been in the household for at least five years. Two-thirds or more had been bought new in state shops; of the re-mainder, roughly half were bought secondhand, and half obtained as gifts or legacies. Holdings of the other items (armchairs, carpets, and sideboards) were less common, as they were not so easily acquired; and they were more likely to be acquired from secondary sources. About half of the families had no armchair (!), the main reasons for its absence being not wanted (30.7 percent); no money to buy one (33.3 percent); and nowhere to put it (35.3 percent). The shortage of living space and presence of 2.3 beds in each dwelling give credence to the last response. Carpets, which pose less of a spatial problem, and are a traditional sign of well-being, were owned by about two-thirds of the families, but desired by nearly all. Most people blamed their absence on a lack of funds. Of the families without a sideboard (about a quarter), all wanted one; but some could not afford one, and others had no space.

The value of furniture may vary considerably according to circumstance, and assessment of that value is no easy matter. Responses indicated a range from virtually bare rooms at one extreme to a respectable degree of ac-coutrement at the other. The central 90 percent of our sample, however, re-turned figures of between 120 and 1,000 rubles.

Holdings of other domestic goods were fairly extensive and roughly matched the urban averages published for the late 1970s.[15] The goods, however, again tended to be old. Generally between a quarter and a half of them were bought secondhand or procured without payment; sewing machines, pianos, antiques, and jewelry were more likely to be acquired by gift or legacy. The main reasons for absence were the householders' lack of interest in acquiring them and a lack of funds to do so. All in all, the figures for furniture and domestic goods suggest a state of cramped and meager adequacy, though there was obviously considerable unfulfilled demand.

If a fair assortment of articles was to be found in households with so low a per capita income, several explanations may be proposed. The official ethic vaunts a high standard of living and encourages the acquisition of domestic equipment. The development of heavy industry is not unconducive to the production of "heavy" household goods. Long-term deficits of other consumer goods have no doubt engendered corresponding emotional responses, encouraging acquisition as taking advantage of an opportunity "not to be missed" and the longer use of personal property. As for electronic devices, the authorities have always evinced a strong interest in the spread of radio and television sets for propaganda purposes. The high incidence of refrigerators reflects the need to preserve scarce foodstuffs, while the possession of sewing machines has been encouraged by the high cost and shortages of clothes. Thus does Soviet reality impose its own exigencies on the contents of people's homes.

Food Purchases

The assessment of food by means of a survey such as ours encounters certain difficulties, the most important of which need to be mentioned at the outset. First, individual tastes may vary enormously, so that items purchased in large quantities by one household may be quite unwanted in another. Second, some comestibles are seasonal and can only be bought for a few weeks of the year: some should be available all the time, but are not, as a consequence of supply failures. It is not easy to distinguish between these items in a typical month's purchases. Third, the number of different foodstuffs bought is normally great and (unlike the contents of a wage packet, for example) cannot always be easily remembered. Many families buy some of their meals outside the home, and it is hard to fit this kind of consumption into any comprehensive pattern. My main effort is therefore directed to illustrating, on a fairly general level, procurement and costs of important staples, leaving aside foods that are consumed rarely or in small quantities.

Foodstuffs Purchased

Table 3.15 gives the sample returns over a fair range of comestibles, most quantities being recalculated to show per capita purchases in pounds, ounces, or pints over a week. It will be noted that the range of vegetables bought in any quantity was very narrow; through the winter months some 52 percent of the households bought no salad, and 25 percent no fruit. The large quantities entered for fresh berries (over 78.0 percent of the sample bought them) is explained by the brevity of the season and the shortage of other fruit and vegetables. Much of the soft fruit is traditionally preserved as jam or compote for the winter.

We endeavored to assess meat purchases not only by quantity, but also by quality, which is ignored in official sources. Overall meat consumption was, as might be expected, quite low. But if the total of the purchases is taken as 100 percent, only 23.6 percent was held to be of good quality; 43 percent was of average quality, or mixed; and 34 percent, including the cheaper salami, was of poor quality. Nearly half of the respondents did not give any figure at all for good meat. The small quantities of vegetables and meat were balanced by relatively high figures for fish, cheese, and other milk products. Most of the milk is consumed in the form of yoghurt, milk concentrate, cottage cheese, and the like; fresh milk is often difficult to obtain, while the heavier cheeses are expensive.

The families were asked about their purchases of a number of more costly, but not luxury, commodities. These were: tinned vegetables, citrus fruit, bananas, preserves, pastries, and coffee. As one might expect, the quantities reported were tiny, and many families did not buy them at all. It is probable that the purchase of some fruit and sweets was prompted by the presence of children.

Purchases of alcoholic drinks were, as may be seen, very moderate: 45.4 percent of the families said they drank no spirits; and 17.2 percent, no wine or beer. The adult vodka drinkers among them averaged only 0.53 pints (0.38 liters) a month, while wine and beer drinkers consumed 1.4 pints (0.66 liters). These rates, to judge from other responses (see table 3.15 below), are far from typical. But the popular view that Jews, who made up the great majority of the sample, on the whole drink less than gentiles may well be correct, and, moreover, anyone planning to emigrate would presumably have had extra incentive to control expensive habits. When asked to estimate how much vodka and spirit the "average worker" drank, most respondents entered between one and three liters a week, with a median estimate of 1.5 liters (or 3.1 pints). This is an extremely heavy rate, even for the USSR, and would have cost around 70 rubles a month. I suspect, therefore, that it may have been attributed to "heavy" rather than average drinkers.

Table 3.15   *Purchases of Foodstuffs*

Kind	Quantities (lbs-oz, per capita, per week)[a]	Percent of sample buying	Principal sources[b]		
			State shop only	Collective-farm market only	Both
Fresh vegetables, cabbage, beetroot, onion	1-04	99.4	41	16	41
Other fresh vegetables for cooking	0-06	92.8	42	17	40
Salad vegetables, summer months	1-12	98.3	25	23	49
Salad vegetables, winter months	0-06	48.3	52	27	18
Apples and pears, summer months	1-14	99.7	25	24	50
Apples and pears, winter months	0-09	84.8	62	18	19
Fresh berries, summer months	1-05	78.2	—	—	—
Meat of all types, fresh and preserved:					
a) Good quality, poultry, dry salami	0-08	52.6	31	56	5
b) Average quality, mixed	0-14	97.9	68	19	12
c) Poor quality, bone, gristle, fat	0-06	69.3	88	10	1
Boiled salami, sausage, ravioli-type products	0-06	94.0	91	3	2
Fish and fish products, fresh and preserved	0-06	94.8	68	10	21
Eggs (number)	(3.4)	97.7	78	8	12
Butter	0-05	100.0	—	—	—
Oil	0-04	99.7	—	—	—
Milk, liquid milk products (pints)	(2.6)	99.4	—	—	—
Cheese, cottage cheese, and like products	0-08	99.1	76	11	12
Sugar	0-09	99.7	99	—	—
Bread and bread products (macaroni, flour, biscuits; pastry excluded)	3-14	100.0	99	—	—

Table 3.15   *(continued)*

| | | | Principal sources[b] | | |
Kind	Quantities (lbs-oz, per capita, per week)[a]	Percent of sample buying	State shop only	Collective-farm market only	Both
Potatoes	2-13	99.4	44	4	40
Tinned preserved vegetables	0-07	72.9	—	—	—
Oranges, lemons, bananas	0-05	80.5	—	—	—
Preserved fruit, berries, jams, and the like	0-06	74.3	—	—	—
Pastries, etc.	0-04	75.9	—	—	—
Coffee	0-04	46.3	—	—	—
Vodka and spirits (adults only, pints)	(0.53)	54.6	—	—	—
Wine and beer (adults only, pints)	(1.40)	82.8	—	—	—

[a] The figures given refer to weights, unless another kind of measurement is indicated within parentheses.
[b] Source figures are to the nearest percentage point. With regard to sources of supply, the table does not give data for products not usually bought at a market, nor for marginal sources of supply.

The list of quantities shown in table 3.15 represents items said to have been purchased at retail outlets, not necessarily consumed. A full estimate of consumption would, on the one hand, have to allow for deterioration (especially in the case of vegetables), inedibility, and wastage. On the other hand, certain other sources of nourishment would have to be added. The first is, of course, meals taken outside the home: 71.5 percent of the families took a median of 25.6 meals per month at work; most of the children in educational institutions used school dining rooms, which in a normal month would have meant an approximately equal number of meals per child. Meals served in the cheaper catering establishments would tend to be of rather poor quality, however. Smaller additions would include food filched at the place of work; gifts from family or friends; berries or mushrooms collected in the wild; occasional products from hobbies like fishing; and produce from the odd garden plot (of which, incidentally, there were three in the sample).

Some Comparisons of Consumption

The consumption patterns of the Soviet poor assume most interest when compared with those of other groups in the USSR or abroad. This exercise raises great methodological problems, not only because of the purchase/consumption distinction, but also because Soviet consumption data are set in broad, largely unexplained, categories. I have, however, attempted a simple recategorization of the sample purchases for this purpose, and the comparisons obtained are worthy of scrutiny (table 3.16).

Despite all efforts to order the sample figures in the most advantageous manner, they lag far behind the declared national averages.[16] The gap cannot be closed, even when some allowance is made for food obtained from the secondary sources noted above. The configuration of the poverty food basket in the late 1970s would appear to match national consumption rates of a decade and a half earlier and betoken a meager degree of sufficiency. It was way behind U.S. levels and even further from the "perspective," or long-term minimum, proposed by Soviet scholars. A question that it raised but left unanswered was the relatively small quantities of bread, potatoes, and sugar entered by most respondents in the sample. These are the items, in my view, that are most likely to be supplemented by cheap outside meals; however, they may have been underreported because they were taken for granted, or because a high consumption of such simple fare was thought to look bad. On the other hand, the Soviet consumption figures for these foods are known to be inflated by kilos purchased illegally for animal feed. Hopefully, underreporting of the consumption of bread and so forth does not affect the validity of other conclusions regarding poverty consumption patterns.

Sources, Costs, and the Popular Response

Information on where the sample families purchased certain products is also presented in table 3.15. As may be seen, frequent use was made of the collective-farm market, indeed a fair proportion of people bought some items only there. This practice was certainly encouraged by supply difficulties. An inability to buy important foodstuffs was reported by almost 90 percent of the families, the great majority entering a frequency of three to twenty instances a month. The reasons for this were not so much a lack of money (7.8 percent of the replies), as an absence of goods in the shops (33.1 percent), or a combination of the two (58.8 percent). Unfortunately, the collective-farm markets have two well-known drawbacks for poor people. They are few and far between, and, more important, prices in them are nor-

Table 3.16 *Food Consumption Patterns*
(per capita, per annum; in kilos)

Foods (Soviet categorization)	(1) "Minimum" poverty diet (1965)	(2) Average Soviet per capita consumption (1965)	(3) Average Soviet per capita consumption (1979)	(4) Average per capita consumption, USA (1979)	(5) "Perspective" poverty diet (mid-1970s)	(6) Poverty sample (median purchases)
Meat, meat products, animal fat, conserves	44.0	41.0	58.0	120.4	75.0	38.4
Milk and milk products	146.0	251.0	319.0	151.2	184.0	289.5
Eggs (units)	124.0	124.0	235.0	283.0	153.0	130.4
Fish and fish products	23.0	12.6	16.3	6.1	19.8	8.8
Sugar	30.0	34.2	42.8	41.4	40–44	12.0
Vegetable oil	16.0	7.0	8.4	12.2	10.0	5.4
Potatoes	137.0	142.0	115.0	66.6	126.4	59.8
Vegetables	121.0	72.0	98.0	89.2	164.0	60.0
Fruit and berries	28.6	28.0	38.0	62.2	81.0	31.8
Bread, macaroni, flour	145.0	165.0	139.0	89.9	174.0	90.0

SOURCES: G. S. Sarkisian and N. P. Kuznetsova, pp. 58, 105ff., 139ff. (columns 1, 5)
Narodnoe khoziaistvo SSSR v 1979, p. 432, 1980, p. 405 (column 4)
Statistical Abstract of the United States (1981), p. 126 (columns 2, 3).

mally from 2.0–2.5 times higher than in state shops. Obviously, a poor person on a tight budget would not choose to buy market goods, were goods of comparable quality available in the state sector. Use of the markets could only have raised the families' expenditures for food and exacerbated their financial difficulties.

Costing the food basket takes us into an even more difficult dimension. Any estimate here involves not only quantities, but also seasonal price variation and source. Costs, it must be remembered, may vary from nil, for gifts, pilfered, or home-grown items, to a considerable sum, when it is a matter of food bought in the collective-farm market. Although rigorous assessment of all such outgoings is impossible, I would propose two fair estimates. The first is the global sum entered by the respondents themselves: nearly all assessed their outgoings, excluding outside meals, at between 15.0 and 53.0 rubles per head monthly, with an average of 33.7 rubles. The second assessment is my own, based on the cost of individual items entered by 120 families who chose to give detailed estimates. The range in this case was somewhat wider, but yielded an average figure of 35.4 rubles. The cost of eating out averaged an extra five rubles per capita per month over the whole sample.

The negative implication of food costs running at these levels hardly needs to be labored. They must have absorbed some 72 percent of official income, or 64 percent of total income as assessed above. Such figures are much above the levels postulated in the "ideal" minimum budgets of the mid-1960s and are high by any Western standards.

The popular response to all of the difficulties as described, a long-standing feature of Soviet reality, is again of particular interest. I decided to pose a question on satisfaction with family food, rather than on shortages, so as to determine people's attitudes, as it were, at the dinner table. No one expressed himself or herself as "very satisfied," but 28 percent of the respondents were "satisfied," and another 10 percent had no opinion on the matter. This left some 50 percent who were "rather dissatisfied," and 12 percent who were "very dissatisfied."

The balance, in our opinion, is rather intriguing, and raises the question of why so many people were unconcerned by what would, in most consumer-oriented countries, be regarded as an intolerable situation. The most probable explanations are simple habituation and the deflection of public interest from dietary matters. Such processes are, of course, greatly eased by the exclusion of information about relative abundance in other lands. A more sympathetic interpretation would be that people who were "satisfied" had greater success in obtaining produce that was in short supply; but the sample returns produced no evidence of this.

Clothing for Adults

Clothing has long been a problem in the USSR, mainly on account of frequent shortage and high cost. Here, again, there was a virtual silence in Soviet sources. The sample results indicated that by the late 1970s, despite improvements in production and some fall in prices, clothes were still a major cause of concern for poor people.[17] The problems of analysis are again great, but I decided that some generalization would be feasible on the basis of a subgroup of 260 males aged between 30 and 50, that is, people who would need only adult clothing but be less disposed than, say, a younger or female group to indulge in heavy spending on fashionable garments. In fact, only 8 percent of this subgroup expressed a keen interest in clothes; about half were rather interested, and the rest were not interested or actually neglected their dress. Yet, despite the predominance of relaxed attitudes in this regard, over two-thirds declared that clothing was an "acute" problem, and nearly all of the others said it was an "average" problem.

Holdings of basic garments are illustrated in table 3.17. This suggests a distinct shortage (given the severe Russian climate) of such key garments as winter coats, fur hats, and light coats. Indeed, some people could only have managed at all by borrowing from relatives or friends. Holdings of other items (some not mentioned in table 3.17) were at least adequate. Only a small portion of the heavier garments was new and many had been heavily worn or repaired. A fairly large proportion of light coats, sweaters, fur hats, and mackintoshes were, it will be noted, purchased in secondhand shops. Very few respondents admitted to accepting them as gifts or hand-me-downs.

Estimates of expenditure on clothes were difficult to analyze, as they were extended by relatively indifferent individuals at one extreme and by a few apparent fashion-seekers at the other. However, some 95 percent of the subgroup entered figures of between 25 and 170 rubles a year, with a mean of about 85 rubles. This works out to around 7 rubles a month, or 11.5 percent of the average total income.

Educational Attainment

Education in modern society is essential for occupational advancement. This is particularly so in Soviet-type economies, where the state authorities control almost all responsible posts and the qualifications needed for them. Ave-

Table 3.17 Wardrobe of an Employed Male
(per capita holdings of principal items)

Item	Median number owned	% of respondents not owning any	Condition of Garment		Number bought in commission shop
			Heavily worn	New or as new	
Winter coat	1.01	22.3	12.4	2.0	4.4
Fur hat	1.05	25.4	29.2	9.9	23.8
Short/light coat	1.24	12.3	20.0	15.7	24.1
Mackintosh	1.27	8.8	10.8	9.9	17.0
Suit	2.21	0.0	5.5	16.7	7.7
Jacket	1.51	5.0	19.6	14.7	8.1
Trousers	2.72	0.0	10.6	28.1	3.1
Sweater	2.03	6.9	20.5	15.5	22.8
Pairs of shoes	2.78	0.0	8.9	16.3	3.5

nues of advancement for persons without recognized certification are correspondingly restricted. It is interesting, therefore, to assess the involvement of our sample in the education movement that has swept the USSR in recent decades.

The returns in fact suggest that the overwhelming majority of the 480 children in the sample benefited considerably. The extent of coverage by age group may be judged from table 3.18. Some 57 percent of the 1–5-year-olds were enrolled in preschool establishments, a figure which probably approached the national average (official data series have not so far been made available). In the largest towns almost all children in this age group attended such establishments, but the smaller towns, where many of the sample families lived, were less well served. The figure for the enrollment of the 6–7-year-olds in schools was lower, because this is a transitional age group between preschool and primary school.

Eight years of full-time general schooling, though modest by international standards, was in the late 1970s still the core of the Soviet educational system. As may be seen, 93.4 percent of the sample children in the relevant age groups were attending these classes, and another 3.2 percent were in other types of educational institution. A nonattendance rate of 3.3 percent is not insignificant, but may be explained by such factors as illness, family disruption, and so on. It would appear, at any rate, that among these families negligence and truancy were minimal.

As for further schooling, only eight respondents said that they had children who had not been able to continue to study although they had wanted to do so. All of them gave financial problems as the main cause. It is only fair to add, however, that four of the youngsters concerned had failed entrance examinations.

Employment is possible under Soviet law from the age of fifteen, but we find that only 2 of the 20 fifteen-year-olds, and 9 of the 50 aged 16–18 (inclusive) were out earning. However, 48 of the 50 were still engaged in some form of full- or part-time study. Of the 33 aged nineteen plus, two-thirds were working, but 30 were also continuing their studies.

Despite this rather impressive picture, it is significant that those who went on to further education did not seem to get into the most desirable institutions. Thus, of the 27 persons continuing study beyond the 10-year school, 3 were in lowly vocational colleges, and 3 in SSUZÝ. Of the 18 who were at VUZy, only one attended a university (the most prestigious type); 5 were in (unprestigious) pedagogical institutes; and 3 were in part-time courses of study.

These figures indicate an intense concern with educational attainment, and I incline to the belief that it derives in part from the education-oriented

Table 3.18 Educational Status of Children in the Sample
(percentages of given age groups)

Age	No school	Nursery	Incomplete general	Complete general	PTU	SSUZ	Incomplete higher	VUZ
1–5 years	43	57	—	—	—	—	—	—
6–7 years	19	44	37	—	—	—	—	—
8–14 years	3.3	—	93.4	2.2	0.5	0.5	—	—
15 years	—	—	48	40	8	8	—	—
16–18 years	—	—	—	72	6	14	—	4
19–26 years	—	—	3	15.6	9.4	—	12.5	44

Table 3.19   *Why Poor Children Have Worse Educational Chances*
(reasons offered as "very important" or "important"; absolute figures)

Reasons	Very important	Important
Parents' lack of necessary connections	166	36
Parents' inability to bribe	108	75
Parents cannot afford coaching	98	86
VUZy favor privileged children	68	95
Poor children are badly schooled	17	59
Other reasons	1	5

nature of the sample. At the same time, there was a widespread feeling in the sample families that "poor" children in general did not have a fair chance of academic advancement. Thus, of the 248 respondents who answered the question, no one thought that a poor child's chances were better than those of the well-off-child; 3 percent thought they were the same; 80 percent thought they were worse; and 17 percent thought they were much worse. The explanations given most often involved, perhaps not surprisingly, poor parents' lack of influence, inability to pay bribes (not necessarily money, it would seem), and inability to hire private tutors (table 3.19). Most of those responding thought that the general schools did not usually vary substantially in the social composition of their pupils and were not to blame for this phenomenon.

As for continuing education among the parents themselves, only 21 out of 442 respondents were involved in it over a three-year period preceding their departure from the USSR. The studious came from all income brackets, but were mostly drivers; possibly the flexible hours associated with that kind of work made it popular among those who wished to continue their education. Ten of the 21 were (somewhat surprisingly) still attending part-time incomplete general school, while 7 more were in PTUs. Two were registered in full-time agricultural VUZy (traditionally having the lowest entry requirements), while 2 were in military colleges. The pattern of educational involvement in the second generation was therefore poor, in contrast to that of the younger generation.

Social Mobility

Social mobility is an extremely complex topic, to be defined and measured in many ways. Here I shall consider only four of the most tractable, which have to do with occupation and educational attainment. They are (*a*) inter-generational mobility patterns; (*b*) respondents' progress during their working years, as perceived by themselves; (*c*) differences between spouses, insofar as they reflect social distance; and (*d*) respondents' views on the ordering of jobs according to a prestige hierarchy. Income changes, another dimension commonly analyzed, are less meaningful in the Soviet context, and income range was, in any case, deliberately restricted for the purposes of this study.

Social mobility as reported by emigrés should normally be treated with caution. This is not because their accounts are likely to be less reliable in this respect than in others, but because any long-term plans that they had for change in the socioeconomic status may have been unconsciously influenced, many years in advance, by the intention to leave their homeland. Fortunately, though caution is still apposite, other sample responses suggest that respondents were only marginally affected in this way.

Intergenerational Mobility

A simple, schematized overview of movement of son as compared to father, and of daughter as compared to mother, in the spheres of occupation and education is given in tables 3.20 and 3.21. The numbers are too small to justify subtle mathematical analysis, but even at this level of generalization some interesting features emerge. Let us begin with movement upward.[18]

In the sphere of occupation, movement was considerable for both sexes. Only about a quarter of the men and a fifth of the women remained in the same category as their parent of the same sex. Upward mobility was more common than downward mobility for both sexes. If the number of down-wardly mobile persons is subtracted from those who were upwardly mobile, without reference to extent of movement, we have a preponderance of 24.4 percentage points for upward mobility among men and 43.2 among women. The apparent difference between the sexes may be explained, at least in part, by the lower job status of women in earlier decades and recently increasing opportunities for them to work outside the household. The more detailed figures suggest, logically enough, that the downwardly mobile of both sexes tended to have parents in higher occupation categories, which were perhaps harder for the offspring to match. The fact that higher occupations usually

Table 3.20   *Intergenerational Mobility (Occupation)*

	Males			
	Working parent	Retired parent	Total	Percent
Son +2 categories or more	26	64	90	40.0
Son + 1	6	15	21	9.3
Same as father	20	38	58	25.8
Son −1	6	16	16	7.1
Son −2 or more	10	40	40	17.8
Total, males:	68	157	225	100.0

	Females			
	Working parent	Retired parent	Total	Percent
Daughter +2 or more	17	45	62	49.6
Daughter +1	1	14	15	12.0
Same as mother	8	17	25	20.0
Daughter −1	3	7	10	8.0
Daughter −2 or more	3	10	13	10.4
Total, females:	32	93	125	100.0

NOTE: Categories are the same as those listed in Table 3.5.

take longer to enter does not invalidate this observation, for most sample members were of an age to be well advanced in their careers.

Upward mobility seems to have been even more marked in education, a finding that reflects, of course, well-documented government policies. Here only about an eighth of the men and a fifth of the women remained in the same category as their parent of the same sex. Around 60 percent went considerably further, and few failed to match parental achievement. The educational levels registered by respondents are, for obvious reasons, likely to be more definitive than are their occupations. The overall picture, though resting on a small numerical base, again indicates a plausible measure of positive change.

As for downward mobility, the amount in occupational terms is particularly interesting when viewed against the movement in education. Although only 3.7 percent of all respondents had a lower educational attainment than a parent of the same sex, 23.7 percent were lower in occupational terms.

Table 3.21   *Intergenerational Mobility (education)*

	Males			
	Working parent	Retired parent	Total	Percent
Son +2 categories or more	23	58	81	60.9
Son + 1	23	2	25	18.7
Same as father	**15**	**18**	**16**	**12.0**
Son −1	4	3	7	5.3
Son −2 or more	4	0	4	3.0
Total, males:	69	64	133	99.9

	Females			
	Working parent	Retired parent	Total	Percent
Daughter +2 or more	70	27	97	63.0
Daughter +1	11	9	20	13.0
Same as mother	**0**	**31**	**31**	**20.0**
Daughter −1	1	1	2	1.3
Daughter −2 or more	1	3	4	2.6
Total, females:	83	71	154	99.9

NOTE: Eight categories are recognized as follows: no education (category 1); incomplete secondary education (2); complete secondary education (3); PTU or low-grade technical schooling (4); secondary special technical schooling (5); part-time, or incomplete, higher education (6); complete higher education (7); postgraduate education (8).
A few persons engaged in evening and part-time courses of casual nature were assigned to category 4.

Thus does the growing discrepancy between the occupation structure and educational attainment (long a topic of debate among Soviet sociologists) express itself among low earners. Education does not appear, even in the longer term, to guarantee upward, or inhibit downward, occupational mobility.

Mobility in Personal Careers

When the respondents were asked for an assessment of change in their socio-occupational status during their last year of normal residence in the

Table 3.22   *Reasons for Failure to Obtain Promotion (percentages)*

Reasons	Very important	Important	Not important
Prevented by ethnic prejudice	22	33	45
Lack of education or specialist skill	19	38	43
No suitable jobs	15	47	39
Prevented for political reasons	6	19	75
Unwillingness to promote a woman/ mother of a small child	4	24	72
Prevented for personal reasons	4	11	85
Family circumstances	3	24	73
Health	2	9	89
Age	1	8	91

USSR and during the five years preceding it, none indicated a "marked" improvement, and only 14 percent said there was some improvement. Seventy-five percent saw no particular change, or had difficulty in pronouncing on the matter; 11 percent perceived some, or a marked, deterioration. Generalization over the whole sample is precluded by the diversity of age, sex, and occupation; but a comparison of the first and last jobs of a subgroup (108) of 40–50-year-olds, who may be thought of as the first generation to start a career after Stalin, revealed an equally disappointing pattern.[19]

A comparison of the occupation groups of people declaring improvement with those declaring deterioration provides no clear explanation for differing fates: movement in each case may have been due to the interplay of unique circumstances. Opportunities for promotion may sometimes be actively constructed; on the other hand, the mere existence of such opportunities may encourage competitive attitudes. Certainly, some 61 percent of the upwardly mobile showed real interest in professional advancement, as against 36 percent among the downwardly mobile. Far more of the "succeeders" had a positive estimate of their chances.

Respondents who had desired promotion but failed to get it were asked to assess the main kinds of obstacles they had encountered. It would appear that they had some difficulty in doing so, but the pattern that emerged is shown in table 3.22. The only reasons commonly thought to be important were ethnic prejudice (that is, anti-Semitism), a lack of skill, or the absence of suitable jobs. Politics, it will be noted, were almost discounted.

Although the years of rapid social change in the USSR are long past, it would still be possible, in theory, to postulate a perceptible fall in the number of poverty-related jobs and some turnover among the people who did them. Furthermore, some obvious poverty-generating factors that plague other societies—such as intense unemployment and large families—are not characteristic of Soviet European towns. The survey results, however, indicate a substantial degree of occupational stability among persons in low-paid jobs in the late 1970s, which contrasts markedly with the intergenerational mobility that preceded it. In the absence of evidence to the contrary, this limited finding lends support to the belief that Soviet society has developed its own poverty trap. Significantly, only about 3 percent of the respondents believed it was easier for poor people to better themselves in Soviet society, while 55 percent believed it was harder.

Marriage Partners

The selection of a marriage partner is as much an emotional as a social act. Nevertheless, the occupational and educational gaps between spouses remain a useful gauge of social mobility, even when ethnic constraints (such as characterize our sample) are taken into account.

The differences between spouses in these terms are set out in table 3.23. The same categories are used as hitherto. With regard to occupation, choice of partners appears to have been fairly open. Although husbands showed a fair disposition to marry someone in the same or an adjacent occupation

Table 3.23   *Comparison of Husband and Wife by Occupational and Educational Categories*

	Occupation		Education	
	Number	Percent	Number	Percent
Wife 4 or more higher	10	3.2	3	0.9
Wife 2–3 higher	46	14.7	69	21.5
Wife one higher	53	16.9	56	17.4
Husband and wife in same category	52	16.6	103	32.2
Wife one lower	61	19.5	46	14.3
Wife 2–3 lower	60	19.2	43	13.4
Wife 4 or more lower	31	9.9	1	0.3

NOTE: Same categories as used in tables 3.20 and 3.21.

group (53 percent of the couples were in this type of union), 47 percent chose wives from a group further away. At the same time, some imbalance may be perceived at the extremes of the distribution, insofar as wives were more likely to be in lower-grade jobs than their husbands. This follows from the generally higher occupation ratings of the husbands.

The educational match, on the other hand, was different. Nearly two-thirds of the husbands took a partner from the same or an adjacent category. In cases of great discrepancy, however, a larger proportion of wives tended to be more highly educated than their husbands. A comparison of these imbalances may indicate some career deprivation for the more educated women, or less insistence on having a career. Clearly, though, it would be wrong to leap to simplistic conclusions solely on this basis.

Low-Prestige Jobs

Given the reluctance of the Soviet authorities to permit sociological listings of the poorly paid jobs, I decided that the opinions of the sample would be well worth having. The nature of the interview made it impracticable to ask for scaled assessments, so respondents were asked to enter instead what they thought to be the four least prestigious occupations in the USSR, together with probable wage rates for them. I made the simple assumption that the more often a job was named, the less it was valued among poor people generally. In fact, the frequency distribution of the 1,638 entries was much more peaked than I had anticipated, which indicates a considerable degree of consensus.

Table 3.24 lists unprestigious occupations entered twelve times or more by order of frequency. As may be seen, all of them were thought to be low-paid; most were believed to yield only 50–100 rubles a month. The detailed ordering of the entries is arguably less important than their general configuration, insofar as a few jobs that are less common, and some that are far down in the list, could well be regrouped with similar ones higher up (for example, stokers are rather akin to laborers, and buffet managers to waiters, and so forth).

Beyond this, the list speaks for itself. Nearly all of the jobs included were in the service sector, involving unskilled tasks like cleaning, carrying, and guarding. The fact that they are also among the least prestigious in bourgeois society may be taken as some demonstration of the ineffectiveness of six decades of egalitarian propaganda.

The less lowly jobs in the list deserve comment. Cashiers, waiters, and buffet managers may have been included on account of the reputation they have for pilfering or theft. The same may be true for checkers, packers, and

Table 3.24 *Low-Prestige Occupations, with Assessed Wage*

	Number of responses	Likely earnings[a]	
Occupation		Range	Average
Cleaner	273	55–90	70
Watchman	150	55–100	72
Unskilled worker	134	50–100	78
Sweeper	96	50–120	72
Nurse (unskilled)	73	55–90	67
Loader	69	60–100	78
Dishwasher	40	50–90	69
Cashier	36	60–120	77
Checker	35	60–100	76
Waiter	29	60–90	70
Lift operator	25	50–80	64
Stoker	25	60–100	76
Packer	22	60–100	76
Courier	20	60–80	67
Postman	20	60–80	72
Bus conductor	20	60–90	72
Tailor, seamstress	20	60–100	76
Warehouse worker	19	60–90	71
Nurse (skilled)	17	60–120	68
Laundrywoman	17	60–80	68
Horsecart driver	16	60–80	69
Deliveryman	14	65–90	77
Buffet manager	12	60–80	71

Total number of responses = 1,182
[a] Rubles, monthly

warehouse workers. Nurses evidently suffered from the low status officially accorded to medical services. It is noteworthy that the only productive workers to appear, apart from general laborers, were those involved in garment making. Given the low pay in some branches of industry, one might have expected to find other production jobs there as well. It would appear that any possible improvement in the popular image of leading industrial workers had not, by the beginning of the 1980s, reached other manual workers or low-grade service personnnel.

Perceptions of Poverty

To what do poor people in the USSR attribute poverty? In order to elucidate opinions on this matter, the questionnaire listed 26 likely causes, divided into two broad groups: those that might explain poverty as generally observed, and those that could account for hardship in the respondent's own family. Respondents were asked to state whether they considered each factor "very important," "important," or "not important," with an extra option added for indecision. The configuration of replies, shown in table 3.25, was in many respects rather as might be expected. But there were also one or two surprises.

The general factor thought to be important, or very important, by most respondents (87 percent) was alcoholism. The prominence of this explanation in the public mind evidently reflects the extent of the evil. The aftermath of the Second World War was thought by many to be an important cause of poverty, which reflects both the actual impact of the tragedy and the insistent projection of it in official media. Economic failings of the government thought to be most blameworthy included incorrect wage policies; the absence of material incentive, which reduced desire to work; high prices for consumer goods; official neglect of agriculture; and the emphasis on militarization.

All of these factors are, of course, interrelated and may engender poverty in any industrialized society. It is, however, curious that so many people should also blame Soviet foreign aid (despite positive treatment of it in the media) and geographical conditions. Few people blamed temporary dysfunction of the economic system, genuine defense needs, or Russia's historical backwardness. The least mentioned (but not negligible) factor was hostility on the part of the West, though people who ultimately decided to emigrate would naturally return a low rating on that point. It would appear, incidentally, that our listing was thought to be fairly complete, because only 2.5 percent of the sample found it necessary to add comment of their own.

The personal, or family, factors mentioned with greatest frequency were incautious procreation, the choice of a poorly paid trade or profession, and lack of education or training. It is hardly surprising that respondents should have been unwilling to admit such failings as lack of initiative or an inability to handle money. What is interesting, and speaks in favor of the sociopolitical "normality" of the sample, is the low rating accorded to the remaining choices. Few people attributed their material hardship to a lack of desire to make a career in the USSR; to their having made overt criticism of Soviet power; or to a lack of interest in material things. Again, only a handful of respondents entered factors beyond those listed.

Table 3.25 *Common Explanations for Poverty*

	Very important	Important	Not important	Cannot say
General Factors				
Alcoholism	44	43	11	2
The consequences of the war against Hitler	38	32	18	12
Wrong government policy regarding pay	36	46	9	9
Absence of material incentive	35	37	23	5
Unjustified high prices for clothes, consumer goods, and services	31	64	4	1
Neglect of agriculture by the authorities	30	52	5	12
Soviet aid to developing countries	25	61	3	11
People's unwillingness to work, lower productivity	23	45	26	6
Geographic, climatic factors, harvest and transport failure	21	56	16	8
Official policy regarding armaments	21	35	20	24
Temporary dysfunction of a good economic mechanism	4	30	24	42
A real need to strengthen national defense	4	15	41	39
Russia's historic backwardness	3	14	47	36
Hostility of the West; its unwillingness to trade	1	23	42	34
Personal Factors				
Family size	24	52	22	2
Choice of a low-paid specialty	20	32	36	12
Lack of a specialty or of education	18	20	55	8

Table 3.25   (*continued*)

	Very important	Important	Not important	Cannot say
Unwillingness or in-ability to find extra income	2	23	68	7
Reasons of age or health	3	15	77	6
Hinderances to promotion at work	2	20	67	11
Lack of interest in material things	1	6	81	11
Unwillingness to make a career in the USSR	2	8	84	6
Feckless handling of family income	0	6	75	19
No known sources of extra income	0	12	80	8
Overtly critical attitude to Soviet power	3	5	82	10
Chance misfortune, illness	4	12	80	5
Other personal factors	4	1	26	70

The degree to which people in the sample, given their admittedly low incomes, *felt* themselves to be poor is another aspect of the problem. Our sampling experience left no doubt that in the USSR poverty evokes negative reactions quite familiar to people living in capitalist lands. Moreover, it is a condition that even people critical of the regime are reluctant to admit having experienced. The interviewers found it desirable to avoid using the word "poor" when asking respondents about their life-styles and advised its removal from the title of the questionnaire.

Despite low living standards right across the sample, only about 2 percent of the respondents admitted to being "very poor," and another 20 percent to being "poor." Some 13 percent thought they were not poor at all, regardless of their admittedly low income, while the remainder, nearly two-thirds, said they had either not thought in those terms or had difficulty in replying. Respondents were asked to state whether, as a consequence of their "low income," they ever experienced a condescending attitude on the part of officials. The responses here were "often" (3 percent); "sometimes" (1 percent); rarely, or not perceptibly (74 percent). Opinions on whether the

Soviet urban poor formed a separate social group were split almost equally three ways among those who thought they did, those who thought they did not, and those who had no comment.

A further explanation for reluctance to admit any degree of apartness emerged when we sought opinions on the *extent* of living conditions similar to the respondents' own, as subjectively perceived. Nearly three-quarters considered that between one- and four-fifths of the populace shared their difficulties.[20] Moreover, when asked to estimate the Soviet average wage in the late 1970s, no less than 99 percent of the respondents entered figures considerably lower than those officially published, the median estimate being 129 rubles, in contrast to 163.3 rubles in the 1979 official statistical handbook. Given the nature of Soviet statistics, one might hesitate to defend the latter.[21]

It seems fairly clear from the pattern of replies that most people in the sample would admit to no clear-cut or pervasive feeling of alienation. I incline to the opinion that there is little, at least at the level of deprivation considered here. Although Soviet society is far from homogeneous, it lacks the variety that pluralism, freedom of expression, and market forces promote. Soviet man may well find that the shared experience of Soviet reality, to the exclusion of any other, strengthens rather than weakens feelings of social cohesion.

Since all respondents had, of necessity, experienced life in the United States or Israel, we asked whether they thought "material difficulties" were easier to bear under capitalism than under socialism. The economic problems of resettlement would, of course, have varied from one respondent to another, but I judged them common enough to justify a general question. The responses were not as unanimous as one might have expected. While about three-quarters of the respondents thought poverty was indeed more tolerable in the West, some 3 percent thought such problems much easier, and 10 percent easier, to bear in the USSR. Fourteen percent said there was little difference.

No treatment of poverty in the USSR would be complete without a few words on begging. This practice, so shameful in an avowedly socialist state, has received little or no attention from analysts in the USSR or abroad. Casual observations made by our respondents, and their views on the "ideal" beggar, are therefore not without interest.

No less than 46 percent of the sample declared that they saw beggars from time to time, the great majority of these respondents reporting between 2 and 30 sightings a year. Only one person, however, admitted to a personal acquaintanceship with a beggar. The most common locations for begging were given as streets, suburban railway stations, and cemeteries. Beggars were thought to be, in the main, poorly educated, unskilled men, or elderly people of either sex with little or no pension. Estimates of their income ranged between 20 and 40 rubles a month; however, a fifth of the respondents entered figures of between 45 and 80 rubles, high enough to have unnerving implications for the character of poverty in general. Begging, like unemployment, finds no recognition in Soviet social-security legislation, and vagrancy, which is ill-defined, has been prosecuted with some vigor.

The most common reason for begging, given by about a third of those who had observed beggars, was physical incapacity, although a quarter named both low wages and drunkenness. Unemployment ranked very low as a reason, being entered by only 2 percent. Interestingly, ten respondents (some 4 percent) entered drug addiction, which is now, it seems, attracting more public attention. Beggars' clothing was assessed by nearly all who completed the entry as "badly worn" or "ragged." The practice adopted by some American beggars of donning a nice suit so as to earn the pity of a more opulent clientele has yet to find a place in Soviet reality.

4 | Poverty and *Glasnost'* in the Press

A Preliminary Overview

There is little doubt that the least privileged people in the Soviet Union have, in the past, tended to suffer worse than others from the ubiquitous censorship system. Investigative journalists were long prevented from treating them as an identifiable social group or describing their problems. Extracts from a censor's handbook published for closed distribution, probably in 1970, listed many relevant prohibitions. They applied to such topics as the distribution of wages and incomes, the purchasing power of the ruble, alcoholism, drug addiction, occupational injuries, the incidence of crime, vagrancy, prison populations, illiteracy, and mass accidents.[1] The list may sound astonishing, but anyone who has perused the Soviet press with any regularity can vouch for its accuracy. The plight of the poor was by this means concealed from public view, and they were robbed of opportunity for airing well-justified complaints.

Since coming to power, Gorbachev and his closest associates have consistently emphasized the need for a better public understanding of existing difficulties. The code word for all of this is, of course, *glasnost'*, or openness in the media. This policy has naturally attracted much attention in the West. It involved the partial breaching of many prohibitions and offered much promise for the future. At the same time, it had not (at least up to the time of the Nineteenth Party Conference in July 1988) brought anything like the openness that characterizes the media in the West, where by and large considerations of national security, public morality, and defamation alone constrain public utterance. Thus, the official 1987 statistical handbook broke relatively little new ground in the pattern of its contents. A curious Soviet analysis of newspaper articles in 1986 estimated the volume of critical items in some national dailies to be as low as 8 percent of their total output, *critical* being used, of course, in a narrow, Soviet sense.[2]

The Soviet leader's condonation of more openness nevertheless lifted a corner of the veil of secrecy that had shrouded many socioeconomic problems. The most significant aspects of this policy, from the point of view of underprivileged members of society, included the cautious resuscitation of poverty studies by academic researchers; the tolerance of more extended and critical comment from specialist Soviet observers; and the reporting of striking individual cases in the press. It is perhaps fitting that we conclude our study of deprivation in Soviet society by considering topics of this kind, for they illustrate what could, and what could not, be said. Let us begin with the matter of poverty studies as such.

New Research on Poverty

The background to the concealment of problems of poverty in Soviet society is a matter I have considered elsewhere.[3] With the "Stalinization" of the media in the 1930s, the very word *poor* was banned from official documents as a description of any social group or condition in the land. Information on family budgets continued to be collected in great quantities, but economists and sociologists were apparently not allowed access to it and were certainly prohibited from publicly discussing the problems that it posed. The situation improved only after the 22d Congress of the CPSU in 1961. Subsequently, as part of Khrushchev's liberalization campaign, systematic study of so-called minimum family budgets was started in a number of Moscow research institutes. Some models were actually published in 1967, and though they were in some ways methodologically suspect, they did at least permit tentative scholarly quantification of a major social evil. The ban on the word *poverty* was circumvented by using the euphemism *maloobespechennost'*, meaning underprovision, as a working substitute.

But what began as a promising branch of social research soon withered. The most important cause for this was the fact that even the most modest threshold prescribed by the analysts for that period (just over 50 rubles monthly for each member of a small urban family) required that two people be earning a wage that closely approximated to the published national average.[4] The new Brezhnev leadership was too conservative and suspicious to allow free expression of so distressing a matter. After the mid-1970s living standards, as I have noted earlier, ceased to rise and probably fell, which exacerbated problems of poverty. Although Gorbachev's policies, unlike Khrushchev's, have not so far been specifically poverty-oriented, it was perhaps inevitable that the new general secretary's concern with living standards should have reactivated this branch of social research.

In September 1986, V. Kriazhev, a veteran in the study of living standards and head of the "Living Standards" division of the USSR Research Institute of Labor, published an article revealing that research work was again in progress. A year later I. I. Gladkii, chairman of the USSR State Committee for Labor and Social Questions, declared that a new minimum budget would become operative (whatever that meant!) in 1988. It appears that a number of institutes were involved in the research, and that at least two budgets—a minimal and an optimal—were being worked out. They would be state-approved (rather than merely academic) and cover different demographic groups and regions. Depending, then, on the progress of *glasnost'*, we may or may not have a selection of poverty thresholds to ruminate over in the fairly near future.[5]

These thresholds will also, it seems, be very Spartan and modest. The interpretation of poverty discussed by Kriazhev seems to be exceedingly conservative and indeed close to the ideas of the 1960s. He held that a per capita income of 60 rubles a month was still an acceptable marker. Some adjustment was possible, he said, according to the circumstances and geographical location of the family, but the figures would then range from 50–90 rubles.

In addition to his comments on the poverty threshold, Kriazhev made some proposals for the general direction of policy regarding the alleviation of poverty. As for poverty among the working population, help should be based not on some principle of social justice or given through automatic access to social consumption funds (for example, via education, health care, and the social-security system). Rather, a solution should be found through increasing opportunities for the able-bodied to make a bigger contribution to output and thus earn a more ample reward. The phrase he coined was "increasing the level of material well-being on a labor basis."

Kriazhev proposed the creation of new trade-union entities called "commissions for work with underprovisioned families," representing all sections of the staff of any given enterprise. Their tasks would be to single out such families; help their unemployed members to find work—full-time, part-time, or home-based; ease possible difficulties at home (by placing children in day care, for example); and maintain contacts with local employment bureaus. Family members who were already employed could be given better-paid jobs, chances for further training, extra work, overtime, and so forth. All of these changes should, however, fit the enterprise's production plans.

As for the nonworking poor, social consumption funds should be used as before, eligibility and minimum payments being adjusted when necessary. It would, however, be wrong to think in terms of free handouts (like gifts for children) because, apart from the difficulties of implementation, this would engender bad attitudes, such as wastefulness, abuse of the gifts, and theft. Any help should take the form of rubles. More effort should be made to give poor children a good start in school, especially in such spheres as sport and music, and in out-of-school activities. As for one-parent children, a minimum maintenance should be introduced (which was in fact done). Other means of assistance could be the increased output of cheap goods, though without detriment to quality, specially extended credit terms for the low-paid, and more help in developing household plots. Kriazhev's proposals obviously cannot be taken as a blueprint for the future, but their emphasis on more work, self-reliance, and efficiency undoubtedly bears a strong Gorbachev coloration.

To return to the matter of the poverty threshold itself, if current thinking proceeds no further than Kriazhev's statements, that would be unfortunate. The inclusion of even low estimates for annual inflation would mean that Kriazhev's threshold was considerably lower, in real terms, than that proposed over two decades ago, and that government help would, by the same token, be restricted to an ever poorer circle of recipients. A 50- or 60-ruble per capita cutoff point is, of course, still used in determining eligibility for certain state benefits, while the full old-age pension for peasants is only 40 rubles.

The apparent adoption of such a threshold has, however, been criticized in the Soviet Union both directly and by implication on a number of occasions. The economist A. Malov, writing in October 1987, declared that the threshold should be 75–80 rubles (as an average over the whole country). A statistical note in the 1987 national statistical handbook, which went to press in August 1987, delineated an income group with less than 100 rubles. This was probably given as a round figure, but it also indicated a threshold or distinct step in income distribution. The study of occupation groups with just over 100 rubles per capita by the sociologist T. Z. Protasenko revealed that between 40 and 50 percent of them found this sum hardly enough to manage on. Further, a man by the name of M. Mamedov, writing to *Izvestiia* from Baku, was quoted as saying that even "100-ruble families" spent 80 percent of their income on food, and 10–15 percent on other essentials—"so you can count up how much is left."[6]

Beyond this, there has been a renewed interest in the so-called rational budget, one which provides a fully adequate level of sufficiency. The eminent sociologist L. A. Gordon, writing in April 1987, stated that the current average wage of 196 rubles, though guaranteeing a standard of living above the poverty threshold, was only half of what was needed for rationality. He was, it appears, referring to a recent definition of the rational budget that required a per capita income, not of 60, but of 200 rubles a month for the average urban family. This would seem to be an updating of the "rational norm" of 135 rubles proposed in the 1960s.[7]

Given the nature of these comments, can anything further be said about the extent of poverty in the USSR in the late 1980s? Despite some slight improvement in the provision of published statistics, the information available is still very disappointing. The 1987 statistical handbook did not break any new ground in this respect; many observers—not all of them non-Soviet—had hoped for the appearance, at long last, of rudimentary tables of wage or income distribution. Alas, nothing of the kind was provided. The handbook did, however, reveal that the proportion of population with per capita incomes of 100 rubles or less was about 35 percent. The true significance of this figure cannot be assessed, because no details were given about its provenance. The 1982–1983 Leningrad survey quoted by Protasenko showed 18 percent of the townspeople to have a per capita income of 80 rubles a month or less. Occasional, but revealing, comment may be printed in Soviet newspapers.[8]

Given the undertakings in hand, and the advance of *glasnost'*, one is loath to venture into the sort of hypothetical calculations about the extent of poverty that were justified some years ago. My own feeling, however, is that if we now take as the poverty threshold a family per capita income of around 80 rubles, for both town and country, then the projections we made for the late 1970s—that up to two-fifths of the population were (by Soviet standards) living in poverty—may still be close to the truth.

Specialist Comment

The more relaxed publication policies have meant that persons with specialist knowledge have been able to draw public attention to poverty-related problems and suggest remedies. I use the term *poverty-related* in this discussion with some care, insofar as overt and extended treatment of the poor as a social group still seems to be some way off. Even Kriazhev approached the problem only from a technical and administrative angle. More incisive discussion of specific social issues has appeared, however, and hopefully will extend further as time goes by.

The writers who attract most attention tend to belong to the liberal wing of Soviet social science, and they have provided much of the work already chosen for comment in these pages. Nevertheless, the fruits of *glasnost'*, particularly those containing suggestions for alleviating deprivation, deserve further illustration. The three examples I have chosen for that purpose include Academician Tatiana Zaslavskaia's criticism of restrictions on social information and proposals for involving sociologists in social reform; Nikolai Shmelev's startling comments on the lamentable state of the economy and his suggested remedies; and the journalist Anatolii Rubinov's discussion of unannounced price rises, which are an extremely sensitive matter for many people. The section concludes with some results from an unusually bold questionnaire distributed through the literary journal *Sel'skaia molodezh'* (Rural youth).

In February 1987, Academician T. I. Zaslavskaia, who is reportedly close to Gorbachev, published a long and outspoken article in the newspaper *Pravda.* Though devoted primarily to the state of Soviet sociology and its role in *perestroika,* she had quite a lot to say about the harm done to the study of social problems by censorship.[9] The USSR, she said, was far behind many countries, including the "most advanced," in the publication of statistics on negative social phenomena. This was to be regretted, because full information about all social spheres was essential for making proper decisions, of which the new economic reform required "hundreds and thousands." Sociologists, she asserted, should have a voice in this extraordinarily important matter.

She proceeded to criticize the USSR Central Statistical Administration (C.S.A.), in a manner possibly unique in post-Leninist history, for keeping its "storehouses" of data closed to outsiders. Since the latter half of the 1970s, she wrote, the development of social statistics had come to a stop. The administration's failure to publish data from the 1979 All-Union Population Census was but one example. Since then, ever new areas of social information have been closed to qualified analysis.

Data about crime, suicides, alcoholism, drug abuse, and ecological damage have not been published, though these topics have long been an object of statistical study in economically developed lands. Much the same could be said about migration and the incidence of certain kinds of sickness. Why, she continued, was information on the differentiation and structure of personal incomes and general well-being published so sparingly? Would it not be better to focus public attention on negative trends and discuss the best solutions? This is precisely what the reorganization of social relations, as proposed at the 27th Congress of the CPSU in 1986, would bring about.

The collection and internal analysis of social information had expanded systematically, but, contrary to the policy of *glasnost',* learned bodies were getting even less data from the C.S.A. than they had before. Zaslavskaia said that she had personally come up against restrictions with regard to the orientation and the content of her work. There were periods when "it was probably simpler to enumerate the things that could be studied than those that were not recommended." These restrictions had to be removed if sociology was to make effective recommendations on painful and pressing social problems. If people were denied information about their own living conditions, they could not be expected to be active either in the sphere of production or in politics; nor could they respond truthfully to official appeals. The restrictions that Zaslavskaia listed were, interestingly enough, close to the list in the censor's handbook that we have just referred to.

Zaslavskaia also complained about the exclusion of sociologists from the solution of social problems. Indeed, it would be difficult, she said, to name any governmental decision in the social sphere that was based on reliable sociological research. Mistakes that had been committed as a result included the legal pressures on the household plot in the early 1960s; the unjustified reorganization of collective farms into state farms; the dispiriting division of rural settlements into those with, and those without, a future; the construction in rural localities of unpopular high-rise apartment houses; the closure of small rural schools, and so on. The absence of any proper "dialogue" between sociologists and administrators was harmful to both sides.

If appeals like Zaslavskaia's are successful and result in the publication of better statistical series, or in trusted scholars having easier access to data banks, Soviet society stands to benefit greatly. The "if" is a big one, since adequate revelation could only fuel further doubts about the success of Soviet social engineering and its function as an exemplar for other lands. Rather than lose so valuable a propaganda tool, many Soviet officials would no doubt prefer a reassuring silence.

Nikolai Shmelev's article in the June 1987 number of the literary journal *Novyi mir* attracted immediate attention at home and abroad. Although concerned with the mechanics of economic regeneration, the article related closely to social problems, and it is from this angle that I shall summarize the content. Shmelev began by declaring boldly that no one could be satisfied with the state of the Soviet economy, which was unbalanced and hardly manageable. There was a purely administrative view of economic problems, and a senseless reliance on pressure, slogans, and coercion. The present desperate situation had come about partly because of the monopolistic position enjoyed by the productive forces in a situation of universal deficit, and partly through lack of interest in technical progress.[10]

The USSR had one of the lowest rates of productivity in the modern world. The most "patriotic" reckoning suggested that only 17–18 percent of Soviet manufacturing-industry output matched international standards, but a more cautious one would take the figure down to 7–8 percent. The task of the current five-year plan was to get it up to 80–90 percent, but attainment of this level was uncertain. Analysts should admit that the problem of "consumer choice" was one of technology, competition, and public attitude, with absolutely no odor of ideology to it. Proper answers could be ar-

rived at only by lively discussion, rejection of the past, and fertile cooperation. A complex socioeconomic system needed self-tuning, self-regulation,
and self-development.

In Shmelev's view, adequate social motivation was essential for economic
success. Workers had lost interest in honest, conscientious work; theft, lack
of respect for honest work, and aggressive envy of anyone who honestly
earned high wages were common. Drunkenness and idleness had taken their
toll of health and morals. As a result, people had lost faith both in communist goals and the possibility of economic advance. Hopelessness and alienation were rife. This could be changed by a new, "self-financing" type of
socialism, and, although it could take years to get into place, no real alternative existed.

After these rather damning propositions, Shmelev turned his attention to
the problems of Soviet agriculture. The economic decisions taken so far, he
claimed, have been half-hearted and of little use. At least four new initiatives
were needed. First, there must be a firm rejection of the practice of handing
down instructions to collective and state farms and of interfering in their
administration. Second, the prices payable for farm produce should be made
more uniform and higher, so that the losses suffered by such sectors as animal husbandry and potato growing could be eliminated. This would mean
a healthy reduction in state subsidies, which currently exceeded 50 billion
rubles. Third, the relationship between the state apparatus and agricultural
collectives needed further adjustment: there should be a progressive rate of
income tax and complete avoidance (except when absolutely no alternative
existed) of output targets measured in kind. Last, farms should be able to
sell their produce freely, and the output of private plots should be put on an
equal footing with that of the public sector.

Shmelev was very concerned about the need to retain well-motivated
people on the farm. The suppression of the kulaks under Stalin had, he held,
meant the loss of the majority of the best agricultural workers. But a few
remained, and it was essential that their skills and enthusiasm be preserved
and utilized. Unfortunately, the highly desirable policy of encouraging at-
tachment to the land, of reviving the spirit of private ownership and collective enterprise, was being damaged by inept criticism of so-called unearned
income, particularly by left-wingers and bunglers, under the guise of a
struggle for social justice.

Examples of this were an incipient drive against productive household
plots and indications of a pogrom against private greenhouses, gardens, and
private fodder cultivation that appeared in the summer of 1986. It was
absurd that the Soviet Union should buy so much grain and meat abroad,
while the initiative of millions of villagers was stifled. Regrettable, too, were
the crude campaigns against middlemen and the prohibitions against send-

ing local produce to other parts of the country. The choice people faced was between more home-produced food or equal deprivation for all.

Shmelev did not mince his words. Stupidity and Stalinism should be recognized for what they were, he wrote, and rejected. No matter if "ideological virginity," which existed only in "fairy-tale" editorials, was lost. Anyway, the concept of equality of incomes was being abused by the very people who made money without creating anything, and who were incapable of doing so. Far better to encourage those who were willing to work to do so. The problem of limiting high incomes, and preventing them from reaching socially dangerous levels, was a simple one and could be left until later. There was no point in killing the goose that had just begun to lay golden eggs.

The problem of providing enough consumer goods was also acute. The ineffectiveness of the incentives offered to workers at present was due not only to the fact that the economic system itself was bad; there was simply nothing for people to buy with their money when they got it. Saturating the market, and giving the man in the street some choice, would mean that the power of earnings would at last make itself felt, and people would genuinely want to work harder. Here the expansion of the private and cooperative sector in the towns would help. Not only would it supply markets, but it would also generate useful competition for light industry, trade, and the public services. All the necessary conditions for encouraging private enterprise—buildings, land, equipment, and raw material—existed in plenty. On the other hand, the protection that state enterprises enjoyed was an invitation to idleness. The import of widely used goods was too limited to affect them. Such enterprises would either have to improve their work drastically or lose part of their income to other producers. This would mean a decrease in the wages they could pay and less spending by them on social needs. There would also be a reduction in staffing levels, and the closure of entire enterprises was not excluded.

Private enterprise, Shmelev continued, needed some control, otherwise there could be an upsurge of theft and corruption. But such evils could be avoided if there were free wholesale trading in equipment and materials, and if the individual/cooperative sector were subject to the same legal and economic conditions as state-run enterprises. State planning was in sad need of democratization; the massive system, which monitored no less than 24 million items, would have to be simplified. What was needed was more limited, but highly effective, planning, involving no more than 250–300 types of strategic product, and regulation only of the most important budget relationships.

It was, however, in the sphere of employment that Shmelev made his most surprising comments. He referred approvingly to an efficiency experiment that had been conducted at the Shchekino Chemical Combine during the

Brezhnev years. The results had been deliberately ignored by Soviet ministries, but if implemented elsewhere, the method would allow a reduction of 25–30 percent in the work force over one and a half or two years without large-scale investment. This was of particular importance when many branches of industry were running 20–40 percent below capacity, on a one-shift basis, while desperate shortages of manpower were being experienced on the country's building sites.

In fact, fresh public thinking was required with regard to unemployment. It already existed among people who were looking for work or changing jobs: the figure for these could scarcely be less than 2 percent of the work force, or 3 percent if unregistered vagrants were included. People should recognize that some unemployment existed and always would. The millions of vacant posts could be used to bring it down to a minimum, with proper encouragement of retraining schemes, transfers, migration, and so on. Furthermore, people should not ignore the economic harm caused by the "parasitical confidence" in having a guaranteed job, for this only promoted indiscipline, drunkenness, and shoddy workmanship. Fearless discussion was needed of the social and economic gains to be derived from a relatively small "reserve" (i.e., unemployed) work force—one which the state naturally would not leave to the mercy of fate.

Administrative coercion would need to be replaced by purely economic coercion. "The real danger of losing one's job, having to go onto temporary benefits [aid] or having to work where one is sent [was] a very effective cure for laziness, drunkenness, and irresponsibility. Many experts think that it might be cheaper to pay the temporarily unemployed an allowance for a few months, rather than to retain obstructive idlers at the workplace." Shmelev's proposals were so novel in this regard that Gorbachev took the highly unusual step of refuting them in public. When questioned at a polling booth a few days after they appeared, the Soviet leader said that Shmelev's article was made up of two parts, one of which reflected the personal views of the writer; but, as for unemployment, it was unacceptable in Soviet society. Shmelev's references to unemployment pay, however, went unmentioned.[11]

Shmelev delivered a hardly less incisive review of the pricing system. Past practice of centralized price setting, he said, robbed the economy of objective guidelines for comparing production outlays and results. Prices for fuel, minerals, agricultural raw materials, foodstuffs, and public services were extremely low, while those for the products of the machine-building industry, including consumer goods, were inflated. (This, of course, has long been recognized by Western observers.) Both wholesale- and retail-price relationships would have to be realigned to correspond with those obtaining worldwide. The vast sums that the Soviet consumer currently received from the public purse in the form of subsidies could perhaps be returned as supplements to basic wages or personal savings. Yet price changes were an extremely delicate matter, especially if they involved marked rises in the cost of foodstuffs and public services. To avoid a Polish-type outburst, the ground would have to be prepared by frank explanation to the ordinary people.

Shmelev had some further comment to make about wage differentials. The low status accorded to engineers and constructors in manufacturing industry and the fact that they were paid appreciably less than some workers clearly reduced their productivity. Further, the low rates of pay earned by the majority of scientific research workers created mass apathy among them.

Reform of the economic system and greater independence for production enterprises would entail, in Shmelev's view, a shake-up among Soviet managers. They were not answerable to their own staffs, let alone their economic partners. In most respects they were accountable to, and concerned about, good relations with their own bosses. Money bonuses meant very little to them: generally, they measured success in terms of medals, a local people's deputyship, public prominence, an official car or flat, special privileges, a trip abroad, or relocation to a more prestigious position. But if the economy were to become fully self-financing, managers would have to develop fundamentally different attitudes. They would not only have to produce items, but sell them at a profit; keep to schedules and order books; earn their own investment funds; seek their own technical solutions; and find the best products on offer. They would not monitor their workers' or engineers' pay packets to prevent them from earning too much, but encourage them to earn more. They would have to treat the social problems of their staff as a matter of priority, rather than as something to be swept under the carpet.

Shmelev's article not only proposed far-reaching economic reform, but stressed the close relationship between the country's economic and social problems. What the Soviet economy and the public required, he concluded, were not so much more volume as better quality, more intelligent use of resources, and the avoidance of waste. A well-motivated work force, honest effort, and full shops were an integral part of the equation. If these factors were lacking, people would simply not supply the energy needed for economic regeneration.

Our third illustration of authoritative comment is Anatolii Rubinov's treatment of public reactions to undeclared price rises. Rubinov claimed a long-standing interest in the realities of inflation and had done some journalistic research on the mechanisms involved. His text was based on readers' letters and other material systematically collected through the editorial office of *Literaturnaia gazeta*.[12]

"Life is getting more and more expensive," wrote Rubinov. "Everyone knows it, everyone's talking about it constantly." The Central Statistical Administration produced a torrent of social statistics—from the number of divorces in Riga to the length of tram line built in various parts of the land. Such data may be of interest to some, but most Soviet citizens, whether inhabitants of town or of country, regarded the current price index, technically known as the "index expressing relative changes in the average level of the price of goods, chronologically or by district," as a matter of vital importance. Judging from the information available, it would seem that the C.S.A. was unaware of common price rises or of people's interest in them.

Following the appearance in the newspaper of a number of articles on the subject, hundreds of readers had written to prove that prices were in fact going up perceptibly over a wide range of goods and services. Rubinov listed clothing, footwear, laundering, repairs, the public baths, hairdressing, hotels, postage and packing, the theater, museums, and the cinema.

The editors of the paper compiled a manuscript from the letters and sent a copy to the USSR State Prices Committee, the most authoritative body in this sphere. Alas, neither a full nor detailed reply was received. Readers who supplied their addresses were informed that the committee had referred their comments to its local offices, which would write to them in due course. Naturally, Rubinov added, prices did not fall as a consequence of this correspondence; indeed, "some of them surged ever upward, and merrily floated out to sea."

Rubinov blamed the committee for not informing the public about price rises, although it willingly advertised reductions and clearance sales of cut-price or remaindered goods, presenting such practices as being especially conceived for the public good. The decision to introduce higher tariffs, on the other hand—as when the Ministry of Communications gradually increased charges for absolutely all its services—was strictly "not for publication." People were not told why the most commonly used postage stamp went up by 25 percent, who authorized it, or when. The committee also failed to release details about ministerial gains and public losses from this particular measure. In like manner, the public should have been informed through the open press about higher prices for having clothes made, cinema visits, the baths, and women's boots; the price of the latter, Rubinov observed, had probably doubled over the last twenty years.

Some price rises were, of course, inevitable. After all, sources of raw materials and energy tend to get exhausted, or be further removed from the place of use, and the extra outlays had to be compensated. But this was not always the case. Sometimes managements used changed production procedures as a pretext to claim that without price rises, output and financial targets could not have been met. On the other hand, prices did not seem to fall when raw materials got cheaper.

A price handbook put out by the State Prices Committee, declared Rubinov, stoutly denied that any substantial rises had taken place. It showed, for example, that the prices of leather, fabric, and mixed footwear had gone up by a mere one-tenth of 1 percent. Thus, women's leather boots, which cost 70 rubles twenty years ago, were not really on sale for 120 or 140 rubles. A lot of people would very much like to know which department stores were still selling them at the old prices. Indeed, according to the committee handbook, clothes have actually become 2 percent cheaper. The USSR Central Statistical Administration, for its part, stated that between 1980 and the end of 1985 the prices of all goods except alcohol had increased by 1 percent. But the people who took the trouble to write letters to *Literaturnaia gazeta* had observed far higher rates.

Rubinov concluded his long and critical article with a challenge to the C.S.A. Statistics, he said, always tell us about the past, and, at a time of rapid change, the administration had simply been harvesting an old crop. Would it not be a good idea for it to start life over again, and tell the public how the genuine price index had fared since, say, 1986? Accurate accounting was vital to counter the interests of bureaucrats, particularly interests that ran counter to the state and community. If the previous year's price level were taken to be 100, the C.S.A. could announce what had happened to it one year later. If it should rise above 100, then everyone could see which branches of the economy were to blame; if it did not, the branches that controlled prices could be commended.

Rubinov's article appeared in the middle of April 1987, only a few days before the 1987 statistical handbook went to press. True, both the State Prices Committee and the Central Statistical Administration had been given prior notice of the *Literaturnaia gazeta* investigation. Whether there was time for appropriate editing, I do not know; but the fact remains that the handbook retained its former series of state prices, which (if vodka is excluded) actually registered a 0.4 percent fall in comparison with those of 1985. Again, it remains to be seen whether *glasnost'* will dent the statisticians' armor.[13]

Our last example is provided by the results of a survey based on a questionnaire sent to readers of the magazine *Sel'skaia molodezh'* in 1987. The organizer, Grigorii Kakovkin, provided few technical details about it (his approach was essentially journalistic), but he did reveal that some five thousand people had responded, of whom 41 percent were male, and whose average age was 31 years. Detailed analysis of replies had been impossible owing to the lack of a computer; most of the results were published in the form of an elementary listing of percentage responses for the sample as a whole.[14]

The questionnaire was designed to explore readers' attitudes to their incomes, work practices, and associated matters. The results seem to indicate that, although dissatisfaction was widespread, there were great reserves of personal energy, and an evident willingness to improve matters, should the necessary conditions be created. I shall adduce here only the more interesting.

With regard to the central matter of earnings, the poll revealed that 60 percent of the respondents considered that they should be augmented. Just under a third were of the opinion that they corresponded to the work put in, while a modest 9 percent admitted that they were paid more than they deserved. Just over half considered that they had opportunities for extra work in free time, should they desire to make use of them. Seventy-two percent said that they would work better for more money. In response to the question: "If your enterprise fulfilled (or did not fulfill) its plan, how would your wage be affected?" no less than 41 percent said that it would not make any difference. Nineteen percent, however, said that better performance would increase their wage by up to 30 rubles, and 30 percent said that it would be increased by more.

Seventy percent considered that, honest work being taken for granted, people should have different wages, corresponding to the demands of their employment. The fact that 26 percent appeared to believe in a form of equal pay for all is curious indeed and may indicate a popular reserve of opposition to Gorbachev's differentiating policies. The response is, however, not altogether convincing, for the relevant question contained the phrase: "I think that everybody has equal needs . . . ," which may have signaled that an officially approved answer was required.

Some 44 percent explained the fact that people "still work badly" by blaming the economic system. A further 31 percent considered the reason to be a lack of a "production culture"; and 17 percent, a lack of incentive. Some 85 percent thought that the "worker's conscience" was a reliable guarantee of effort and should be nurtured. Over half believed that the Japanese worked well because their system obliged them to, and over a third said it was because Japanese working practices were so advanced. Significantly, no less than 82 percent of the respondents knew of places where it was possible to earn money by doing hardly any work at all.

In the sphere of criminality, respondents considered that the most dangerous phenomena against which one should struggle were administrative crimes (42 percent), bribery (26 percent), and illegal speculation (15 percent). Giving short weight in shops and pilfering were both entered by 8 percent of respondents. Attitudes that might again be described as Victorian made themselves evident insofar as 80 percent thought that it was bad for youngsters to trade on the market, since money spoiled children.

With regard to the simple matter of having money, 29 percent said they honestly liked it; 10 percent did not; and the remaining 61 percent indicated that they were unconcerned. One wonders whether the response did, in fact, reflect a greater incidence of communistic attitudes than would occur in "bourgeois" society. Perhaps the sting of the questionnaire came in its tail; for when asked whether Soviet society was able "to count its kopecks," no less than 97 percent of the respondents held that it could not. The prospects for true socioeconomic regeneration must be dim indeed, if this assessment is accurate.

Readers' Letters

Observance of *glasnost'* among Soviet editors soon extended to the publication of letters from their readers that could not possibly have been printed before Gorbachev came to power. Before I illustrate this phenomenon, however, a few words need to be said about Soviet readers' letters in general. They have rather a curious history.

It seems that the dispatch of personal requests, complaints, and proposals to official bodies assumed particular importance soon after the Soviet system was established. The final disappearance of democratic politics, the abolition of opposition parties, and suppression of a free press meant that often a letter was the only means an individual could use to make his voice heard on a higher plane. Apart from that, Lenin himself actively encouraged workers, peasants, and indeed whole collectives to write letters conveying their justified complaints (in addition to the welcome expressions of political support and proposals for improvement). As time passed, party, soviet, and trade-union bodies and also organs of the press apparently became the recipients of heavy postbags. Mail of this character, of course, was supplemented by a flow of anonymous missives giving malevolent information to the security organs. By the mid-1930s a body of legislation was in place covering the receipt and investigation of petitions and complaints from the public.[15]

Although the matter is veiled in secrecy, Stalinist terror certainly inhibited the pen. Regular publication of readers' letters was still, however, held to be desirable, and in February 1951 *Izvestiia* itself was criticized for not publishing enough of them or dealing with them properly. Things improved, in this respect as in so many others, when Khrushchev came to power. De-Stalinization meant creating the impression that citizens had gained extra means to influence the government and alert authorities to current abuses. On 10 August 1956, the Presidium of the USSR Trade Unions passed a decree criticizing its local committees for not heeding individual complaints and instructing them to take more active remedial measures. It had become a common practice for letters to be ignored or merely forwarded to the authorities in question, sometimes with dire results.

This measure, in effect, marked a reactivation of official policy in this sphere. A great increase in the flow of such missives ensued, and in August 1958 the Central Committee of the CPSU itself issued admonishments about inadequate responses. The improvement of complaint procedures also accorded with Brezhnev's efforts to improve democratic appearances, and new laws were introduced to this effect. An edict of the Presidium of the Supreme Soviet, issued on 12 April 1968, established widespread responsibility among officials, together with procedures, for registration and examination of cases within one month. The forwarding of complaints to the persons named in them was formally prohibited.

Correspondence of this nature reached, it seems, inundative levels. By the early 1980s the written communications sent to officials numbered many millions per annum. In the five years between the 26th and 27th Party Congresses, for instance, the Central Committee alone received 3.5 million; it was reported that a Letters Section was set up after 1976. The media presented a target in their own right. The president of the Union of Journalists, V. G. Afanas'ev, revealed that *Pravda* got about 542,000 readers' letters in 1985 and 622,000 in 1986. Workers wrote 24 percent, the intelligentsia 69 percent, and students 44 percent more than in the preceding year, but "the number of letters reporting persecution for criticism doubled and amounted to thousands and thousands." Occasional comment has suggested that the most responsive province and city newspapers may expect to get up to 20,000 a year each. Usually, two or three members of a newspaper's staff, making up a separate department, read and distribute the letters received according to their content. Presumably, the torrent has little effect, otherwise the face of Soviet reality would long since have changed.[16]

The Gorbachev leadership does not seem to have made any far-reaching changes in the standard procedures, but party decrees on related topics have emphasized the continuing importance of using the media to publicize selected letters. Scores of letters, and journalistic reviews based on them, have reflected popular disgruntlement with specific facets of Soviet reality. Ironically, many submissions have matched or even surpassed *samizdat* writings in their acerbity.

Foreign observers have begun an analysis of this kind of literature, and no doubt a full appreciation of its content will be available in due course.[17] It is arguably still a little early to undertake that task; yet preliminary perusal suggests that editors choose the letters they print according to a number of fairly obvious principles. Some are used to highlight important social problems and put pressure on the relevant authorities to remedy them. The letter from T. I. Kiselova, extracts from which are reproduced below, is an example of this type: *Literaturnaia gazeta* called on no less than five national ministries and a local authority for action on the matters addressed therein.

In like manner, publication of the letter from Comrade Dudareva on the front page of *Pravda* must have been intended to prompt local authorities to improve grocery supplies in hamlets. Other letters, however, seem to be published with the more general intention of allowing unorthodox, though reasonable, opinions or expressions of discontent to be aired for the enlightenment of anyone who cares to read them. Since readers would include the national or local leaderships, the public might be expected to benefit in consequence. But journalistic self-interest also, one feels, sometimes comes into play, in that an editor might hope to increase his readership with the help of a good letters column.

The letters also give some indication of the limits of *glasnost'* with regard to this genre. Although complaints from well-meaning individuals may be published, missives from groups, or anything resembling a petition, still appear to be banned. Radical criticism of whole areas of administration (particularly the political system) is scarcely possible. Laudatory assessments of capitalism, or positive generalizations about the advantages of capitalist social policies, are difficult to find. In addition, the normal censorship rules exclude anything relevant to national security, the activities of the KGB, criticism of leading national figures, and so on, however much concern such matters may arouse. No Soviet letter writer, to our knowledge, has ever criticized Gorbachev. Two other "forbidden zones" that Afanas'ev noted in the above-mentioned speech were failures or near-failures of the space program's projects and ecological catastrophes. In addition, he added, a newspaper could normally criticize individual officials or areas only once, otherwise it would find itself accused of victimizing them.

Although the advent of *glasnost'* has meant that many social problems that were formerly taboo may now serve as the topics of readers' letters, many more, such as religious witness, anti-Semitism, and sexual abnormality, still appear to be completely banned. Publication of a letter implies endorsement of its content by the editor, with the consequent political responsibility. Thus critical comment must be relatively narrow or local in significance, or contain positive elements (like the references, among our examples, to color television). Compared to the practice of past years, the advances are striking; but a long path remains to be trodden.

Sample Letters

I am the mother of five children ranging in age from 1 to 13. My husband and I are both 35.[18]

True, women have the right to a year and a half of maternity leave (only six months of it without pay). But what about the difference between raising a single child and, say, three or four? And then you have your fifth. You sit at home a year, getting 50 rubles a month, then another six months getting nothing, surviving on your husband's income alone. With five children . . .

Until four years ago, my husband's salary was 180 rubles a month. Even when it rose to 212, it was hard to make ends meet. But as an engineer he could not legally hold a second job. Last year he took a job as an ordinary worker and now makes 260 rubles a month. Yet I figure we need 525 rubles a month (75 rubles per family member) to get by, maybe more, when you consider that the children are growing and their clothes are not getting any cheaper.

Recently, my daughter and I began calculating how much money the family spends each day. Food and transportation cost on average ten rubles per day. Our daughter concluded that her father's salary barely pays for groceries. Where does her mother find the money for everything else? For clothes and shoes for seven people, furniture, a color TV, vacations, the movies, birthday presents?

Her mother earns that money through honest labor: She stays at home with the baby and sews. Yet this is a crime, because she sells the things she makes. The work is hard and also degrading: she lives in constant fear of being cited by the police.

I was once arrested and fined 25 rubles. The police informed my employer that I had been detained while selling goods on the private market. What kind of goods, and how I had acquired them was left unsaid. My boss concluded that I was a speculator and fired me.

That was a long time ago. No one ever explained exactly why I wasn't allowed to sew to earn extra money. A few years later I learned that in order to sew at home one has to get permission from the appropriate financial agencies. I tried to get a permit, but some official refused my application on the grounds that I was already receiving a state benefit.

T. I. Kiseleva, Krasnoobsk, Novosibirsk oblast

From *Literaturnaia gazeta*, 1 October 1986; translation, *Current Digest of the Soviet Press* 38 (1986).

100 rubles, 23 years old, foreman: My wife and I together earn on average 250 rubles a month. At the moment (so far), we have one child.

Why does everything in our country cost such a lot? Take one example—food. Occasionally we're given a pay rise—it's an incentive, and it's fine of course, three cheers! But at the same time food and consumer goods are going up in price. People write in about providing furniture and cars for young people—but what are you supposed to buy them with?

---

85 rubles, 20 years old, a cook: It's hard physical work (we carry full 50-liter vats and cut up carcasses). We spend the whole day in a stifling atmosphere, our feet are wet, and we can't sit down for even a moment. It's like that for thirteen hours a day. In my opinion, our wages don't match up to the labor we put in. Maybe it's the hard, low-paid work that makes you "pinch" things. I left college with high marks and a red diploma, but I only earn as much as a kitchen worker. Is that really fair? If we had the equipment, we could work better.

---

160 rubles, 53 years old, agricultural-machinery operator: In answer to your question about "things that you dream of buying in the future," I've written: a color television. You'll think that's nonsense. You'll say that practically everyone has one, and it's easy to get. Well, it's not. I have two daughters, both with higher education. One has graduated and is married, the other's just finishing. That says everything. All these years, the money's gone for their studies, for clothes and food. If I tell you that my girls have gone through college in different towns, you'll see what I mean. And if you add it all up, at today's prices, then you can only *dream* about a color television, because in our house clothes, food, and all the little necessities have to come first.

---

100 rubles, 26 years old, senior accountant: We young people practically live off our parents—they can help us because they get a pension. But couldn't we do it the other way round, so that young people got pensions or grants? Your wages would be your wages, but in addition you'd get a pension until a certain age—say 40–45, when a woman or a man is still recognizable as a human being. Otherwise people work and work until they're worn out, just to get a pension,—and then they don't last long enough to draw the first installment.

I know a lot of old grannies—take my own, for example—who have money sitting in their savings books, but I haven't got an overcoat, and when I ask for a loan, she won't give me one, she doesn't want to part with it, while I run around in freezing weather in an old Italian-made coat.

---

300 rubles, 44 years old, machine operator: Yes, we earn a lot, but look at the work we do!

People say, and rightly: "You don't get paid money for nothing." But that's only what they say. How many people are there who are taken on as machine hands or operators, and earn 250 rubles, but in fact perform the duties of party-committee secretary, shop-committee chairman, Komsomol organizer, or inspector!

And the brigade he's attached to has to fulfill his share of the plan for him. He gets his danger money, but he doesn't even look in at the shop—in case, God forbid, he should breathe glass dust. His hands are soft, with gold rings—but take a look at ours! All scarred, burnt from hot glass, beyond any manicure. If we earn good money, it's at the cost of hard work and health, and I'm not ashamed to say it.

I've never been abroad, but people who have been have told me about it. It's shameful, shameful enough to make you cry. If you give people a travel permit, they ought to take an exam on how to behave while they're there, so that throughout the whole ten days they remember they're Soviet citizens, with a sense of pride and a sense of dignity. Why aren't they interested in the town, or its monuments, why do they go chasing around the shops instead? Again, because they find things that we don't have. And why don't we have them? Because we don't know how to make them, and if we do, we send them abroad as fast as we can. Our own people have to manage with simple, cheap stuff, or even rejects. And so it goes on.

There are four of us. We're 22 years old: a driver, two agricultural machine operators, and a carpenter.

Sometimes we earn 200 rubles, other months, you end up in debt to the state. There's no decent, fashionable clothing here, and the shoes are too awful to mention—there's simply nothing to wear. You feel ashamed to go out in what there is. There's no tinned meat, or tinned milk, etc. We've no decent furniture for our flats.

Our enterprise almost always fulfills its plan, but that isn't reflected in our wages. They say that intellectual work is harder than physical work—well, we disagree with that one hundred percent. Let a mechanic, an engineer, or a boss work like we do for a month, and then tell us which is harder! We could wear holes in the seats of our pants, too—but that's not work. If a working man thinks something up and does it, and the boss accepts it for use, both of them get a bonus, but what is the boss's bonus for? Signing a piece of paper? Why should we sweat our guts out if we're only getting kopecks for it?

From *Sel'skaia molodezh'*, 1987, no. 11:24–26.

Why hasn't the State Price Committee once published data on our minimum maintenance budget? Or on those millions of people who are on the edge of it or below? Surely the committee must know, for example, that the graduates of higher and middle special educational institutions earn only 100–120 rubles? But they start a family all the same, one child appears, then another, and the mother has to quit her job, and spend years at home. Has the committee worked out how many families there are like that, has it estimated how such a family can live on one person's earnings, without help from parents?

A. I. Vinogradov, Moscow oblast

From *Izvestiia,* 29 December 1987.

Hello, dear editors!

It seems to me that not everyone understands the situation that has come about in agriculture. But we are talking about the exclusion and death of a nation. Millions of people left their villages and went to the towns, where they have to live in hostels until they are 30 or 35, cold, nostalgic and drunk.

Those left in the village are even worse off. They don't have their own land, so they are not even peasants. They are rural laborers. And whoever heard of a laborer working hard on someone else's land, or wanting to have children? Why should he? So that they become laborers too? What is the consequence of having the land controlled not by the people who work it, but by officials and bureaucrats? That has led to our agriculture lagging behind the Americans by 3–5 times. I think the redistribution of the land is the most important and primary task.

Iu. Fedin, former peasant

From *Sel'skaia zhizn',* 1987, no. 12:32.

We live in the hamlet of Shakhan in Karaganda oblast. We have three children, the youngest is not yet two. My husband works in the Shakhtinskii mine, and I also work in a mine, but another one. Just now, though, I'm on holiday.

Yesterday was Sunday, and I went out shopping. The older children stayed at home, and the youngest one went with me. I wanted to buy some butter. If you only saw what was going on in the shop! The queue was just as though people were waiting for bread in wartime. How on earth could I get anything with a baby in my arms? I turned around and went home.

Our district has its own chocolate factory that was decorated for its output, but our children never see good-quality sweets. It would seem as though we should be moving to better times, but in our hamlet everything sort of disappears. There's a shortage of wafers, and biscuits as well. And of salami, cheese, *khalva,* margarine, and other things, too. But every year, to judge from the papers, agricultural enterprises increase their output. So where is it, if the shops are empty? It's true you can get tinned fish, thanks to the efforts of the workers in the fishing industry. Meat has also begun to appear, but only in the cooperative shops, and at a very high price.

So just think, how are you to feed a family in such circumstances?

Dudareva, Shakhan

From *Russkaia mysl'*, 4 December 1987; first published in *Pravda*, 23 November 1987.

Notes

Preface

1. See my studies *Poverty in the Soviet Union: The Life-Styles of the Underprivileged in Recent Years* (Cambridge, U.K.: Cambridge University Press, 1986); *Class and Society in Soviet Russia* (London: Allen Lane, 1972); also *Soviet Sociology, 1964–75: A Bibliography* (New York: Praeger Publishers, 1978), written in collaboration with T. Anthony Jones.

2. The original version was submitted to the National Council in May 1985. A cyclostyled copy of it appeared in the *Berkeley-Duke Occasional Papers on the Second Economy in the USSR*, no. 6, June 1986.

Chapter One

1. International comparisons of living standards are difficult (especially when the USSR is involved) and not attempted with regularity. The *Statistical Abstract of the United States* for 1987 estimated Soviet per capita gross national product to be just under 56 percent of that of the United States in 1983 (p. 824). However, Professor Gertrude Schroeder, who has dealt with this problem in detail for many years, has shown that in terms of per capita consumption Soviet levels are much lower. See her contribution to Horst Herlemann, ed., *Quality of Life in the USSR* (Boulder, Colo.: Westview Press, 1987), p. 13. See also note 8 below.

2. See in particular Gorbachev's detailed complaints at the February 1988 plenum of the CPSU. I use the term "Gorbachev's policies" in the present work as a convenient approximation, for the actual alignment of power in the leading party bodies is complex. This usage is justified to the extent that Gorbachev seems to have been dominant in formulating and promoting the policies in question.

Some Western observers hold that inside the Politburo opposition to Gorbachev soon came to center on the figure of Egor Kuz'mich Ligachev, after other figures, particularly Grigorii Vasil'evich Romanov, had been defeated and expelled. However, the scandal-laden expulsion of Gorbachev's associate Boris Nikolaevich El'tsin in November 1987, for unacceptably strong reformist leanings, and apparent differences between the editorial policies of major Soviet newspapers, illustrate the complexity of the situation.

3. *Pravda,* 27 January 1987. The plan and plan fulfillment data in this section are drawn principally from *Pravda,* 20 June 1986; *Narodnoe khoziaistvo SSSR v 1985,* pp. 61–62, 411, 413–19, 480 (hereafter *Nar. khoz.*). See also *SSSR v tsifrakh v 1986,* pp. 179, 182.

4. Deductions from a wage of 218 rubles would include, according to our best calculation: income tax, without relief—approximately 23 rubles; retained holiday pay—19 rubles; trade union dues—2 rubles. Total deductions would amount to about 44 rubles, leaving a residue of some 174 rubles.

5. *Nar. khoz. 1985,* pp. 40, 46, 100; *SSSR v tsifrakh v 1986,* pp. 5, 39.

6. *Nar. khoz. 1985,* pp. 5, 425. For further discussion of these problems, see pp. 56–59 and pp. 80–87 in following chapters.

7. For assessments, see *Radio Liberty (Munich) Research Bulletin* 250/86 (hereafter *RL Research Bulletin*): *Soviet Economy,* vol. 2, no. 1, Jan.–Mar. 1986; *World Outlook 1988* (The Economist Intelligence Unit), p. 69; *Russian Research Center (Harvard) Newsletter,* vol. 12, no. 6, 13 February 1988.

8. Gertrude Schroeder, "Consumer Malaise in the Soviet Union: Perestroika's Achilles' Heel?" *PlanEcon Report,* vol. 4, no. 11, 18 March 1988.

9. Further estimates of the growth of real per capita household consumption for the period 1976–1985, provided by Gertrude Schroeder, are 15.1 percent in the USSR and 23.2 percent in the United States; for U.K. figures, see *Annual Abstract of Statistics* (Central Statistical Office), no. 124 (London: HMSO, 1988).

10. I. Stalin, *Voprosy Leninizma* (Moscow, 1953), p. 367.

11. *Sobranie postanovlenii pravitel'stva SSSR,* 1986, no. 34, statia 179. Note that I have somewhat reordered the content of the decree for easier presentation. A Soviet summary of this complex measure may be found in *Iuridicheskii entsiklopedicheskii slovar'* (Moscow, 1987), pp. 105, 135. For the commentary see *Sotsialisticheskii trud,* 1987, no. 2:93 (hereafter *S.T.*).

12. *Sotsiologicheskie issledovaniia,* 1987, no. 4:17 (hereafter *S.I.*). It is noteworthy that the author of the article, L. A. Gordon, evidently considered this to be too small. Authoritative expositions of the problems, mainly from economic and technical standpoints, may also be found in *S.T.,* 1987, no. 1:7.

13. Reported in *The Independent,* 29 January 1988; *Pravda,* 3 April 1988.

14. *Nar. khoz. SSSR za 70 let,* p. 108; *S.T.,* 1987, no. 12:35.

15. *Sel'skaia molodezh',* 1987, no. 11:26.

16. *S.I.,* 1987, no. 4:3. There are other comparable examples of scholars evading apparently obvious problems. The prominent welfare economist L. Kunel'skii, in a long article purporting to deal with the same topic (*S.T.,* 1985, no. 11:7), also restricted himself to generalizations. The reform was intended, he wrote, to "ensure a more active interplay of economic and social measures. With the help of social incen-

tives to labor, and moral encouragement, it is essential to increase output and effort, and improve quality, while economizing resources." There would be "encouragement for those toilers who made the biggest contribution to the progress of science and technology . . . a different atmosphere in enterprises and work groups." See also the articles by G. Sarkisian in *Voprosy ekonomiki*, 1987, no. 1 : 11, and G. Sarkisiants in *S.T.*, 1986, no. 6 : 3.

17. *Spravochnik partiinogo rabotnika, vypusk 24, chast' II* (Moscow, 1984), p. 179; *Nar. khoz. 1985*, p. 417.

18. *Ekonomicheskaia gazeta*, 1986, no. 42 : 2.

19. "Ukazy Prezidiuma Verkhovnogo Soveta," in *Vedomosti Verkhovnogo Soveta SSSR*, 1987, nos. 34, 224, 337.

20. *R. L. Research Bulletin* (Russian) 93/87, 28 September 1987; *EKO*, 1986, no. 12 : 140; *Nar. khoz. za 70 let*, pp. 434, 448. The real rate of inflation in the USSR is a matter of debate. Official price indexes for recent years have shown overall rises in the state sector of about 1 percent per annum (there are even slight falls if alcohol is excluded). Street prices, however, are undoubtedly much higher than those officially registered, and inflation has probably reached several percentage points.

21. Proposals for a "planned reconstruction of the price system" were listed as being due at that time in the decree of the Presidium of the USSR Supreme Soviet and USSR Council of Ministers of 28 August 1986. As for rents, the basic rates still current go back to legislation of the mid-1920s, when rates of 35 – 44 kopecks per square meter were established (see M. Matthews, *Privilege in the Soviet Union* [London: Allen and Unwin, 1978]), p. 112; *Pravda*, 28 February 1986.

22. *Voprosy ekonomiki*, 1987, no. 1 : 74; see also p. 123 below for further discussion.

23. The texts of the principal laws are to be found in *Izvestiia*, 21 November 1986 and 8 June 1988. See also I. I. Gladkii, ed., *Individual'naia trudovaia deiatel'nost', sbornik normativnykh aktov* (Moscow, 1987).

24. Detailed listings of what were called "craft and trade" activities, together with some of the regulations, may be found in two separate volumes edited by I. A. Azovkin et al., *Kratkii iuridicheskii slovar'-spravochnik dlia naseleniia* (Moscow, 1962), p. 185, and *Iuridicheskii spravochnik dlia naseleniia* (Moscow, 1968), p. 185. Such private enterprise as was registered was greatly reduced in 1960, with the enforced transfer of some activities to local industry. It includes a contingent of persons doing work at home—*nadomniki*.

25. *Planovoe khoziaistvo*, 1987, no. 7 : 87; *Ekonomicheskie nauki*, 1987, no. 3 : 41.

26. *Pravda*, 20 November 1986; *Ekonomicheskie nauki*, 1987, no. 3 : 42; for further consideration of this matter, see page 75. *Planovoe khoziaistvo*, 1987, no. 7 : 87.

27. For a summary of the legislation, see *Iuridicheskii entsiklopedicheskii slovar'*, p. 251.

28. See *RL Bulletin* 298/87, 14 July 1987, for sources and a listing of cases of obstruction. The figures for cooperatives are from M. N. Rutkevich, "Izmeneniia v sotsial'no-klassovi strukture sovetskogo obshchestva v usloviiakh perestroiki," *S.I.*, 1987, no. 5 : 34, and those for state enterprises from *SSSR v tsifrakh v 1986* (Moscow, 1987), p. 209. See also *Sel'skaia molodezh'*, 1987, no. 11 : 23, and the reports in *The*

Independent (British national daily newspaper), 6 May 1988; 25 May 1988. By the beginning of 1989 the tendency to restrict the functioning of cooperatives seemed even stronger.

29. *Planovoe khoziaistvo*, 1987, no. 8:106.

30. V. I. Terebilov, ed., *Kommentarii k zakonodatel'stvu o trude* (Moscow, 1982), pp. 55–59; *Kodeks zakonov o trude RSFSR*, article 33; Blair Ruble, *Soviet Trade Unions* (Cambridge, Engl.: Cambridge University Press, 1981), p. 68.

31. N. S. Malein et al., eds., *Sbornik normativnykh aktov po khoziaistvennomu zakonodatel'stvu* (Moscow, 1979), pp. 85, 126; the text of the July 1987 law is taken from *Izvestiia*, 1 July 1987. This law was supposed to come fully into effect only after January 1988. Readers should note that I consider only certain social aspects of it in these pages. More general views of its implications and contradictions are to be found in *Radio Liberty Research Bulletins*; see John Tedstrom, "Soviet Economic Performance in 1987: Stumbling Along the Path of Reform," *RL* 60/88 (11 Feb. 1988), and Terry McNeill, "Gorbachev's First Three Years in Power: Reform and Its Prospects," *RL* 75/88 (29 Feb. 1988). The law will be very difficult to implement without, for example, reforming the system of realistic prices.

32. *Spravochnik partiinogo rabotnika, vypusk 26* (Moscow, 1986), p. 426. The educational references are from M. Matthews, *Education in the Soviet Union* (London: Allen and Unwin, 1982), pp. 62, 146.

33. Ibid., p. 428.

34. *S.T.*, 1987, no. 2:93.

35. These regulations, too, have a long and tortuous history. An abridged translation of the present version, entitled "*Tipovye pravila vnutrennego trudovogo rasporiadka . . . 20 July 1984*," may be found in my *Party, State and Citizen in the Soviet Union* (New York: M. E. Sharpe, 1989).

36. *S.T.*, 1987, no. 2:53; *Novyi mir*, 1987, no. 6:154.

37. *S.T.*, 1987, no. 2:53.

38. *S.T.*, 1987, no. 9:5. The 1987 number of *Narodnoe khoziaistvo*, incidentally, showed that the numbers of "conditionally released" persons (presumably dismissed, re-employed, retrained, etc.) in industry rose from 304,000 in 1981 to 536,000 in 1986. The definition is so vague, of course, that the figures are not very meaningful.

39. *Nar. khoz. SSSR za 70 let*, p. 108; *S.T.*, 1987, no. 10:123; 1987, no. 12:35.

40. *S.T.*, 1981, no. 7:64; 1987, no. 4:33; *Argumenty i fakty*, 1985, no. 29.

41. *Iuridicheskii entsiklopedicheskii slovar'* (Moscow, 1987), pp. 156–58, 312–17, 336–37.

42. For the relevant legislation, see E. L. Frolova and L. A. Egorova, *Posobie po sotsial'nomu strakhovaniiu i sotsial'nomu obespecheniiu* (Moscow, 1986), p. 168; *Spravochnik partiinogo rabotnika, vypusk 26* (Moscow, 1986), p. 497; *Nar. khoz. 1985*, p. 415. The rules are very complicated, and we only touch on the most significant provisions here.

43. For a summary of details see *Nar. khoz. za 70 let*, p. 438; and *Iuridicheskii entsiklopedicheskii slovar'* (Moscow, 1987), p. 311. An example of continuing censor-

ship restrictions may be seen in the treatment of the results of a survey of pensioners in *S.T.*, 1987, no. 4:97.

44. A. Solov'ev, "Gotovitsia proekt novogo Zakona o pensiiakh," *S.T.*, 1987, no. 4:79.

45. *Vedomosti Verkhovnogo Soveta*, no. 2, article 34, 1987; no. 43, article 895, 1987; *Iuridicheskii entsiklopedicheskii slovar'* (Moscow, 1987), pp. 22, 233, 336.

46. For biographical details see *RL Research Bulletin*, no. 151/84, 12 April 1984; *Kommunist 1986, kalendar'-spravochnik* (Moscow, 1985), p. 8.

47. *Pravda*, 10 January 1988. *Vestnik agroproma', Ezhenedel'noe prilozhenie*, 2 December 1988, p. 1. For peasant numbers, see *Nar. khoz. za 70 let*, pp. 11, 300. My main concern in this section is to illustrate the circumstances of the peasantry, as such, since state-farm workers are, in the main, covered by "worker and employee" legislation.

48. The total payments to collective-farm members in money and kind rose from 18.8 billion rubles in 1980 to 24.2 billion rubles in 1986 (over a comparable number of farms). *Vestnik statistiki*, no. 7, p. 54; *SSSR v tsifrakh v 1986*, pp. 142, 179, 182.

49. See in particular paragraphs 2, 7, 10, 14, 16–31, 34, and 57–59 statute.

50. B. Zhurikov, *Ekonomika sel'skogo khoziaistva*, 1985, no. 1:3; *Iuridicheskii entsiklopedicheskii slovar'*, p. 195.

51. Two positive instances are described in *Ekonomicheskaia gazeta*, 1986, no. 26, June; Bashmachnikov's article, which we deal with in the next paragraph, appeared in *S.T.*, 1987, no. 5:19.

52. The measures are again too complex for full listing or discussion here, but a detailed account of them, together with evidence of opposition, up to 1986 is provided by Karl-Eugen Wädekin in *Osteuropa*, 1986, no. 1:48–64. For an assessment of the 1987 decrees, see *RL Research Bulletin*, RS 85/87, 3 September 1987. The originals are published systematically in *Resheniia partii i pravitel'stva po khoziaistvennym voprosam* (Moscow, 1977–), vols. 11 onward.

53. An important series of articles in *Ekonomicheskaia gazeta* has served as the basis for these generalizations. See G. Shmelev, 1986 no. 9; F. Bogomolov, 1986 no. 34; A. Drebot, 1986 no. 18; N. Dolinskii, 1986 no. 26; Ya. Glezer, 1986 no. 25; N. Kozlov, 1986 no. 25; B. Bedelov and R. Guseinov, 1986 no. 42. On allotments, see *SSSR v tsifrakh v 1986*, p. 131.

54. *Izvestiia*, 19 July 1987; *Sbornik statisticheskikh materialov v pomoshch' agitatoru i propagandistu*, 1986 (Moscow, 1987), p. 71; *SSSR v tsifrakh v 1986*, pp. 128–31; *Nar. khoz. SSSR za 70 let*, p. 445.

55. *Ekonomika sel'skogo khoziaistva*, 1985, no. 1:31.

56. A model statute for these offices was published in *Ekonomika sel'skogo khoziaistvo*, 1984, no. 7:87.

57. *Ekonomika sel'skogo khoziaistva*, 1986, no. 1:31.

58. *Pravda*, 28 January and 16 December 1987; 5 July 1988. With regard to formal changes in the CPSU since Gorbachev became general secretary, a comparison of the text of the party statutes approved by the 27th Congress in March 1986 with the

preceding version reveals numerous small changes of wording (primarily to accommodate the proclaimed policies on openness, criticism, and improved economic efficiency) but no major modifications. For comment on party elections see the lead article in *Pravda,* 19 February 1988. During the preceding report and election campaign, only about 1 percent of the 426,000 party committees and bureaus were censured for their activities by the membership.

59. *Izvestiia,* 25 June 1987; *Pravda,* 5 July 1988.

Chapter Two

1. For example, the literature bearing on various dimensions of the problem in the United States alone is vast. See, for a review of theoretical approaches, H. Thierry and A. M. Koopman-Iwema, "Motivation and Satisfaction" in P. J. D. Drench et al., eds., *A Handbook of Work and Organisational Psychology* (Chichester, Engl.: Wiley, 1984), vol. 1.

2. *S.I.,* 1982, no. 3:141. See the article by B. Sh. Badi and A. N. Malinkin.

3. A. M. Tikhonov, in *S.I.,* 1984, no. 2:114; V. V. Voronov and I. P. Smirnov, in *S.I.,* 1982, no. 2:16–21.

4. Noteworthy is a 1981 survey of 1,599 young migrants reported by D. I. Ziuzin in *S.I.,* 1985, no. 2:79. The motives most commonly named for departure in this sample were dissatisfaction with wages (45.8 percent), poor living conditions (39.1 percent), lack of promotion prospects (28.6 percent), unsuitable work (29.8 percent), family problems (24.7 percent), conflict with relatives (18.9 percent), and a bad atmosphere at work (13.8 percent).

5. Yu. L. Aranchyn, V. N. Beloshapkina, V. P. Beliaev, and V. I. Boiko, eds., *Sotsiologicheskie kharakteristiki gorodskogo naseleniia Tuvinskoi ASSR. Materialy sotsiologicheskogo issledovaniia* (Novosibirsk, 1982).

6. *S.I.,* 1987, no. 4:65. The family budget data in the statistical handbook for 1983 may in fact show a comparable picture, if the income figures are recalculated to exclude putative state benefits ("free" education, health care, etc.) and a realistic estimate is inserted for expenditure for alcoholic drinks. But the handbook figures are more general. Interestingly, the Latvian study reported by Eglite showed that 17.6–21.1 percent of the sample named a shortage of cash as being first among their daily difficulties.

7. *S.I.,* 1983, no. 2:108.

8. The basic study was conducted in 1962 and selected results were published five years later; see A. G. Zdravomyslov, V. P. Rozhin, and V. A. Iadov, *Chelovek i ego rabota, Sotsiologicheskoe issledovanie* (Moscow, 1967). This book was well reviewed, as marking a great step forward in Soviet labor studies. The results of the 1976 rerun were not, to my knowledge, published in detail.

9. D. P. Jamison, analyst, *RFE/RL Soviet Area Audience and Opinion Research* (cyclostyled), no. AR 1-86, March 1986.

10. *S.I.,* 1983, no. 1:16. We have abbreviated and paraphrased where necessary.

11. *SSSR v tsifrakh v 1986,* p. 218. Soviet sources usually quote figures for "general useful living space" and not "basic" living space as distinguished in the text. The relationship between the two Soviet categories must vary according to circumstances, but as a rule basic living space is thought to comprise 60–65 percent of general useful living space. Hence my approximation. Western statistical compilations usually refer to occupied rooms, or some such concept.

12. *Nar. khoz. 1985,* p. 425.

13. N. P. Moskvichev, *EKO,* 1982, no. 7:171.

14. A. E. Kotliar and M. I. Talalai, *EKO,* 1984, no. 10:138.

15. A. G. Simakov, *EKO,* 1983, no. 7:105.

16. V. A. Iadov, in M. Levin, "Molodezh' i trud," *EKO,* 1983, no. 8:110–28. (A round-table discussion.)

17. V. M. Rutgaizer et al., "K voprosu o reforme sistemy potrebitel'skikh tsen i denezhnykh dokhodov naseleniia," *Izvestiia Sibirskogo otdeleniia A. N., Seria ekonomika i prikladnaia sotsiologiia,* 1987, no. 13:41.

Chapter Three

1. The full questionnaire was a document of 87 pages, divided into three parts. Part A, for completion by the 348 heads of households, contained sections on family composition, income, housing, food consumption, selected expenses, possessions, holiday patterns, household goods, and children's education. Parts B and C, which were identical, were designed for application to one or two working members of the same family, as available for interviewing. These parts covered employment, social mobility, further education, marriage, personal wardrobes, and certain uses of time and elicited repondents' options on the extent and causes of urban poverty in the USSR. Some information was sought on destitute people observed outside the home. The results obtained from acceptable questionnaires were analyzed by means of SPSS programs on mainframe computers. A few questionnaires were rejected as being substandard.

2. The categorization of jobs by content is no easy matter, as has been long recognized. Discrepancies obtain between such elements as physical exertion and manipulative skill; required knowledge and mental agility; administrative responsibility and psychological distance; tedium and initiative.

3. Detailed results of the University of Illinois "Soviet Interview Project" will be helpful in this, as in so many other respects, when they become available. Also relevant are the results of a survey of wage rates conducted in Israel under the direction of Gur Ofer, of the Hebrew University of Jerusalem. There is also a large body of Western scholarship on women's roles in Soviet society based on official sources (see, for example, G. W. Lapidus, *Women in Soviet Society: Equality, Development and Social Change* (Berkeley: University of California Press, 1978).

4. See p. 49 and table 2.6 above. T. Z. Protasenko's findings make an interesting comparison in this regard. In the USSR savings yield only 2 to 3 percent interest. Given this rate and the problems of inflation, savings cannot normally serve as an appreciable source of income.

5. That is, 124 at the workplace plus 160 outside it, minus 69, the number of persons who were in both categories and should not be double counted.

6. The lowest pension recorded in the sample was 12 rubles, and 120 rubles (a state-fixed minimum) was the highest. A distribution of pensions, published in the 1988 statistical handbook, gave no details for those (over half) who received less than 60 rubles a month in 1983, *Narodnoe khoziaistvo SSR v 1987*, p. 398.

7. In 1979 the national average for actual or basic living space in urban areas (see p. 57 and note 11 for chapter 2) was approximately 8.5 square meters per person, calculated as 65 percent of the urban total usable living space given in Soviet statistical compilations. See *Narodnoe khoziaistvo SSSR v 1979*, pp. 7, 418. The figure for respondents living in large towns was, however, only 7.6 square meters.

8. See *Bol'shaia sovetskaia entsiklopediia* (Moscow, 1973), vol. 12, p. 5.

9. *Nar. khoz. 1979*, p. 410.

10. Soviet citizens have a constitutional right to housing (article 44 of the 1977 USSR Constitution) and a fair degree of security of tenure. However, articles 333 and 334 of the RSFSR Civil Code (matched in the codes of other republics) give landlord authorities the specific right to evict without provision of other living space. The principal grounds are (*a*) "systematic violation or spoilage of accommodation, or systematic infringement of the rules of socialist communal living, rendering residence for other people impossible in the same flat or house, after warnings and social pressure have proved ineffective"; and (*b*) (when certain enterprises and organizations let accommodation to their own employees) the tenant's voluntary departure from the enterprise or organization (that is, to take another job), infringement of labor discipline, or criminal activities on his part. It is noteworthy that nonpayment of rent is listed as a reason for eviction only for private lettings. It is not unknown for landlord authorities with ulterior motives to arrange eviction cases deliberately, while the militia may suspend residence rights for certain violations of the law. For the legal texts see *Grazhdanski kodeks RSFSR, s izmeneniami i dopolneniiami na 1 oktyabrya 1978* (Moscow, 1979); *G. K. RSFSR, ofitsial'nyi tekst* (Moscow, 1968), pp. 207–10.

11. Thus 16 and 5 respondents, respectively, reported the building to be in a bad, or very bad, capital state; 31 said the decorative order was bad or very bad; 24, that there were heating difficulties; 32 reported noise; 24, damp; 27, evil smells; 13, poor light; and 26 complained of dirt.

12. G. S. Sarkisian, *Voprosy ekonomiki*, 1981, no. 5 : 12.

13. Prices have risen steadily over the years. See M. Matthews, *Privilege in the Soviet Union* (London: Allen and Unwin, 1978), p. 45.

14. Four families did not specify their accommodation.

15. *Nar. khoz. 1979*, p. 434. Thus, despite their low income, nearly all sample families had a radio, a television, and a refrigerator; just over half had a vacuum cleaner,

a washing machine, and a sewing machine; 34.2 percent had a record player; 22.7 percent, a bicycle; 12.1 percent, a piano. 8.6 percent had some jewelry (but in nearly all cases only one or two pieces).

16. The fact that the national rates are also per capita does not, of course, make them directly comparable with the sample results. But at least the age and sex composition of the sample families is not too distant from the national pattern.

17. Official figures showed that the supply of clothing increased about two and a half times between the mid-1960s (when it was grossly inadequate) and 1980. This presumably meant easier purchase, less illegal price inflation, and greater availability of second-hand goods. State prices fell by a percentage point or two, while the rise in the average wage must also have helped.

18. Although we use the terms father/son, mother/daughter for our discussion here, we are, of course, concerned with the older and middle generations. The relatively low rate of response to questions on intergenerational mobility was a little disappointing, but could sometimes, no doubt, be explained by ignorance of parents lost in the Second World War, by problems of divorce or illegitimacy. It is also possible that some respondents were apprehensive about entering familial details in the questionnaire, despite assurances of anonymity.

The simplicity of tables 20 and 21 should not distract attention from the complexity of the movement behind them. They do not show, for example, the differing occupational and educational structures in which each generation was placed; how far change was personal, and how far due to "structural" development; whether change was greater in some parts of a given occupational or educational structure than in others; how rates changed over time, etc. Note also that my categories were designed to distinguish between job groups, rather than degrees of seniority within any job.

19. Four hundred and seven respondents completed this section. Eighty-two of the 40–50-year-olds had in fact remained in the same category (as defined on my seven-step scale) throughout their careers, and of the 26 individuals who changed, 15 moved up the scale, and 11 moved down it.

20. Poverty in rural areas lay, of course, beyond the bounds of the study, but respondents who had recently been in a village were asked to compare living standards in town and country. Over half refrained from comment, but 10 percent thought rural standards higher; 12 percent thought they were the same; and 25 percent thought they were lower. Since the peasants in most localities had been desperately poor for decades, this assessment doubtless reflected recent rises in their well-being.

21. It is apposite to note that the *Narodnoe khoziaistvo* figures may not be quite what they seem. Soviet employees are paid by the calendar month. However, a prominent Soviet economist has stated that wage figures as published in this source are *nominal*, recalculated to include holiday pay in nonholiday wage packets. Depending on the length of the vacation (which for most people is three–four weeks), the nominal monthly wage packet must exceed the sum actually received by up to one-eleventh. In other words, the published figures have been inflated to include a sum retained to cover the period of annual leave. See V. Perevedentsev in *Zhurnalist*, 1974, no. 8:70; I am grateful to Mr. Keith Bush for this reference.

Chapter Four

1. Though very convincing, the source of this text was never, apparently, disclosed. The actual wording of the most relevant clauses, in poorly edited and imperfect English, was as follows:

Distribution of income and outlays of the all-union budget and the budgets of the union republics; The full wage-fund, or the (money) size of the population's purchasing power, or the balance of income and expendture of the population, or the sum of all incomes of the population by Union, republics, krai or oblast; Distribution of workers and service workers by the size of their salaries; Calculations of the purchasing power of the ruble and of the hard currency of foreign states; [info about victims of various disases including alcoholism, and about invalids . . . x]; The no. of drug addicts by raion, city and higher; Info about professional poisonings and professional illnesses; Information entailing human victims of accidents, wrecks, serious accidents and fires—without the permission of the responsible ministry and department; Info about occupational injuries; Summary data (absolute and relative) characterizing the status of criminality or indictedness (literally—*cudimosti*) of all kinds of crime, including: quantity of crime, the number of people engaged in criminal responsibility, of peope arrested, of those convicted—by region, city and higher; The number of uncared for children, the number of people engaged in vagrancy or begging—by oblast or higher.

For the full available text, see M. Matthews, *Party, State and Citizen in the Soviet Union* (New York: M. E. Sharpe, 1989).

2. The papers were *Komsomol'skaia pravda, Literaturnaia gazeta, Sovetskaia Rossiia* and *Izvestiia,* leaving *Pravda,* in particular, sacrosanct. The articles were categorized as "critical materials on the problems of *perestroika.*" The highest rating was 23 percent. See Iu. A. Kovalev in *S.I.,* 1987, no. 5:80. The 1987 statistical handbook, *Narodnoe khoziaistvo SSSR za 70 let,* the publication of which coincided with celebrations of the seventieth anniversary of the revolution, was part of the usual series.

The main categories of information that were at various times authorized for publication during the first two and a half years of Gorbachev's general-secretaryship included (apart from the social problems discussed here) reports of major accidents, including the Chernobyl' nuclear disaster; public disorder, including a riot in Kazakhstan; occasional data on alcoholism and drug addiction; the release of certain Soviet political detainees; scarcely precedented criticism of administrative failings; news items on the dismissal of certain powerful officials, among them a KGB officer in the Ukraine; occasional dissonant opinions from foreign observers; and criticism of Soviet psychiatric hospitals. Of course, the media maintained many of its traditional silences and continued to turn out a torrent of distorted information about the capitalist world. See, for example, the listings in *Facts on File, Kessing's Contemporary Press Archive,* and relevant *Radio Liberty Research Bulletin* reports, including *RL* 66/87, 23 Feb. 1987.

3. See M. Matthews, *Poverty in the Soviet Union* (Cambridge, Engl.: Cambridge University Press, 1986), p. 7 note, Chapter 1 in general, or "Censorship" in the index; and (with T. A. Jones) *Soviet Sociology 1964–75: A Bibliography* (New York and London: Praeger Publishers, 1978), p. 19.

4. For a detailed discussion of per capita poverty thresholds (51.4 for the mid-1960s, 66.6 for the 1970s), see M. Matthews, *Class and Society in Soviet Russia* (London: Allen Lane, 1972); and *Poverty in the Soviet Union* (Cambridge, Engl.: Cambridge University Press, 1986). The relative stagnation in poverty-budget analysis seems to be demonstrated from the use of the same formulae in discussions of income published in the late 1970s.

5. *S.T.*, 1986, no. 10:91; 1987, no. 12:6; a *TASS* interview of 2 Sept. 1987; *R. L. Research Bulletin*, R. S. 89/87, 15 Sept. 1987.

6. *Argumenty i fakty*, 17 Oct. 1987, nos. 41–42; *Nar. khoz. SSSR za 70 let* (Moscow, 1987), p. 441; *Izvestiia*, 19 Dec. 1987. This argument, as we have seen, is common; see p. 130 and table 2.6.

7. *S.I.*, 1987, no. 4:12. N. M. Rimashevskaia and A. A. Ovsiannikov had proposed a 200-ruble threshold as a minimum in the sense that it allowed a relatively free choice of goods and services. See the references in A. A. Ovsiannikov, *S.I.*, 1987, no. 4:65.

8. T. Z. Protasenko, in *S.I.*, 1985, no. 3:104. A comment in the newspaper *Sotsialisticheskaia industriia* (1 June 1988) by the economist M. Mozhina revealed that a fifth of the population was "at the threshold of underprovision," with an income of 70 rubles a month, while more than half had an income of 125 rubles a month or less. According to *Ekonomicheskaia gazeta* (December 1987, no. 52), some 40 percent of young marrieds in Moscow began life on a per capita income of 50–60 rubles a month.

9. *Pravda*, 6 Feb. 1987. Other interesting articles by T. I. Zaslavskaia may be found in *Kommunist*, 1986, no. 12:63; *Materialy samizdata (Radio Liberty) vypusk 35*, 26 Aug. 1983. We have provided most of the material in this section as précis and fair commentary, rather than in translation.

10. *Novyi mir*, 1987, no. 6:142.

11. *Pravda*, 22 June 1987.

12. *Literaturnaia gazeta*, 15 April 1987.

13. *Nar. khoz. SSSR za 70 let*, p. 480.

14. *Sel'skaia molodezh'*, 1987, no. 11:22.

15. See the decrees of 13 April 1933 and 14 December 1935, noted in *Spravochnik partiinogo rabotnika*, vypusk 9 (1969), p. 404. N. G. Bogdanov and B. A. Viazemskii, eds., *Spravochnik zhurnalista* (Leningrad, 1971), p. 227.

16. For a list of relevant decrees, see *Spravochnik partiinogo rabotnika, spravochnyi vypusk* (Moscow, 1984), p. 248. Further details from *Problems of Communism*, vol. 30, May–June 1981, p. 12.; A. D. Chernev, *Partiinaia informatsiia voprosy istorii i teorii* (Moscow, 1987), p. 125. In 1967 the newspaper *Trud* received 345,000 letters (*Spravochnik partiinogo rabotnika, vypusk 9*, p. 503); see also *KPSS v rezoliutsiiakh i resheniiakh*, vol. 8 (Moscow, 1985), p. 242. For references to readers' letters, see *Zhurnalist*, 1986, no. 9:55; 1987, no. 4:10, 22.

17. *R. L. Research Bulletin*, 391/86, 20 Oct. 1986; 14/87, 8 Jan. 1987.

18. The texts printed here, unless otherwise attributed, consist of brief extracts, sentences, and paragraphs from readers' letters, translated for purposes of our argument. Some of them were published with a signature, others without. In the interest of brevity and easier reading, omissions are not always indicated.

Bibliography

The works listed in this bibliography are those discussed in the text, with some closely related titles added. A few references that are merely tangential to the discussion have been omitted.

Abbreviations: *S.I.* = *Sotsiologicheskie issledovaniia*
            S.T. = *Sotsialisticheskii trud*

Books and Learned Articles:

Aitov, N. "Aktivno vozdeistvovat' no otnoshenie k trudu." *S.T.*, 1982, no. 7: 95–100.

Aitov, N. "Sotsial'no-ekonomicheskaia effektivnost' tekhnicheskogo progressa." *S.T.*, 1985, no. 10: 5–11.

Akhiezer, A. S. Review of *Obraz zhizni v usloviiakh sotsializma (teoretiko-metodologisheskoe issledovanie)*. Moscow, 1984. *S.I.*, 1985, no. 2: 199–201.

Antosenkov, E. G. "Esli proanalizirovat' situatsiiu." *EKO*, 1982, no. 3: 117–20.

Aranchyn, Iu. L.; Beloshapkina, V. N.; Beliaev, V. P.; and Boiko, V. I., eds. *Sotsiologicheskie kharakteristiki gorodskogo naseleniia Tuvinskoi ASSR. Materialy sotsiologicheskogo issledovaniia*. Novosibirsk, 1982.

Artemov, V. A. "Biuzhety vremeni i ikh primenenie." *EKO*, 1982, no. 11: 175–78.

Azovkin, I. A., et al., eds. *Iuridicheskii spravochnik dlia naseleniia*. Moscow, 1968.

Azovkin, I. A., et al., eds. *Kratkii iuridicheskii slovar'-spravochnik dlia naseleniia*. Moscow, 1962.

Badi, B. Sh., and Malinkin, A. N. "Urovni prakticheskogo soznaniia i stil' zhizni: problemy interpretatsii otvetov respondenta." *S.I.*, 1982, no. 3: 141.

Baranenkova, T. "Sokrashchenie tekuchesti kadrov v usloviiakh intensifikatsii proizvodstva." *Voprosy ekonomiki*, 1983, no. 8: 74–84.

Belkin, M. I., and Volkonskii, V. A. "Regulirovanie zarabotnoi platy i interesy proiz-vodstva." *EKO,* 1982, no. 10: 109–28.

Berkeley-Duke Occasional Papers on the Second Economy in the USSR. G. Gross-man and V. Treml, eds. University of California, Berkeley, California; Duke University, Durham, North Carolina.

Bessonova, O. E. "K voprosu o kvartirnoi plate v SSSR (na primere Novosibirska)." *Izvestiia Sibirskogo otdeleniia AN, prikladnaia ekonomika i sotsiologiia,* 1985, no. 1: 57.

Bigulov, B. Kh.; Kryshtanovskii, A. O.; and Michurin, A. S. "Material'noe blagoso-stoianie i sotsial'noe blagopoluchie: opyt postroeniia indeksov i analiz vzaimo-sviazi." *S.I.,* 1984, no. 4: 88–92.

Bliakhman, L. S., and Zlotnitskaia, T. S. "Differentsiatsiia zarabotnoi platy kak fak-tor stimulirovaniia truda." *S.I.,* 1984, no. 1: 39–47.

Bogdanov, N. G., and Viazemskii, B. A., eds. *Spravochnik zhurnalista.* Leningrad, 1971.

Boiko, T. M. "Denezhnye sberezheniia naseleniia." *EKO,* 1982, no. 6: 131–38.

Bolotskii, B., and Golovnin, S. "Razvitie individual'noi trudovoi deiatel'nosti." *Pla-novoe khoziaistvo,* 1987, no. 7: 87–91.

Bozhkov, O. B., and Golofast, V. B. "Otsenka naseleniem uslovii zhizni v krupnykh gorodakh." *S.I.,* 1985, no. 3: 95–101.

Bratishchev, I. "Sotsialisticheskaia proizvodstvennaia distsiplina." *Voprosy ekono-miki,* 1984, no. 10:63–71.

Burov, A. N. "Zarplata—cherez sberkassy: opyt i trudnosti." *EKO,* 1982, no. 11:125–28.

Chernev, A. D. *Partiinaia informatsiia, voprosy istorii i teorii.* Moscow, 1987.

Chizhova, L. "Sbalansirovannost' resursov truda s potrebnostiami ekonomiki." *Voprosy ekonomiki,* 1983, no. 5:61–69.

Dashdamirov, A. F. "Vozrastanie obshchestvenno-politicheskoi aktivnosti kak za-konomernost' sovershenstvovaniia sovetskogo obraza zhizni." *S.I.,* 1984, no. 2:97–103.

Dzhamalova, D. D., and Batygin, G. S. "Sotsiologicheskaia sluzhba gorkoma par-tii." *S.I.,* 1982, no. 1:51–59.

Eglite, P. A. "Osobennosti reproduktivnogo povedeniia v usloviiakh vysokoi vne-semeinoi aktivnosti naseleniia." *S.I.,* 1985, no. 4:59.

Frolova, E. L., and Egorova, L. A. *Posobie po sotsial'nomu strakhovaniiu i so-tsial'nomu obespecheniiu.* Moscow, 1986.

Gladkii, I. I., ed. *Indvidual'naia trudovaia deiatel'nost', sbornik normativnykh ak-tov.* Moscow, 1987.

Gol'denberg, A. I. "Koeffitsientno-dolevaia oplata truda." *EKO,* 1982, no. 2: 131–39.

Gorbunov, E. K. "Normirovshchik mezhdu intensivnost'iu i oplatoi." *EKO,* 1983, no. 9:177–79.

Gordon, L. A. "Sotsial'naia politika v sfere oplaty truda, vchera i segodnia." *S.I.*, 1987, no. 4:3–19.

Grigorian, G. A., and Gukasian, A. Kh. "Kak 'Rabotaet' stimul." *EKO*, 1983, no. 7:72–78.

Gurshumov, I. P. "Motivy potentsial'noi tekuchesti kadrov." *S.I.*, 1984, no. 1: 76–78.

Gusev, Iu. A. *Skol'ko, chto i gde my pokupaem.* Moscow, 1979.

Illinois Soviet Interview Project. University of Illinois at Urbana-Champaign, Illinois (Principal investigator: James Millar). (cyclostyled working papers)

Iuridicheskii entsiklopedicheskii slovar', A. Ia. Sukharev et al., eds. Moscow, 1987.

Jamison, D. P., analyst. *RFE/RL Soviet Area Audience and Opinion Research*, no. AR 1-86, March 1986. (cyclostyled)

Kalinin, V. "Leningradskii eksperiment: chto pokazali sotsiologicheskie issledovaniia." *S.T.*, 1985, no. 4:96–100.

Kissel', A. A. "Tsennostno-normativnyi aspekt otnosheniia k trudu." *S.I.*, 1984, no. 1:47–54.

Kodeks zakonov o trude RSFSR.

Kommunist 1986, kalendar'-spravochnik. Moscow, 1985.

Kostin, L. A. "Reservy ispol'zovaniia trudovykh resursov." *EKO*, 1984, no. 1: 22–38.

Kotliar, A. E., and Talalai, M. I. "Kak zhivet molodoi rabochii." *EKO*, 1984, no. 10: 138–49.

Kovalev, Iu. A. "'Negativ' v presse i effekt bumeranga." *S.I.*, 1987, no. 5:80.

Kovalev, P. "Respublikanskii aktiv: aktual'nye zadachi organov po trudu." *S.T.*, 1985, no. 4:126–28.

Kozlov, A. M. "Kak konstruiruetsia sistema otsenok." *EKO*, 1982, no. 2:124–31.

KPSS v rezoliutsiiakh i resheniiakh. Vol. 8. Moscow, 1985.

Kunel'skii, L. E. "Povyshenie stimuliruiushchei roli oplaty truda." *EKO*, 1983, no. 3:4–12.

Kupriianova, Z. V. "Kak preodolet' defitsit." *EKO*, 1982, no. 3:121–31.

Lapidus, G. W. *Women in Soviet Society: Equality, Development, and Social Change.* Berkeley: University of California Press, 1978.

Levin, A. I., and Rimashevskaia, N. M. "Puti povysheniia kul'tury potrebleniia produktov pitaniia." *S.I.*, 1983, no. 1:44–54.

Levin, M. "Molodezh' i trud." *EKO*, 1983, no. 8:110–28.

Levykin, I. T. "K voprosu ob integral'nykh pokazateliakh sotsialisticheskogo obraza zhizni." *S.I.*, 1984, no. 2:90–97.

Liubomirskii, A. N., and Ialunin, V. I. "Kak premiia prevrashchaetsia v zarplatu." *EKO*, 1982, no. 11:128–31.

Liul'chenko, G., and Toksanbaeva, M. "Povyshenie trudovoi aktivnost." *Voprosy ekonomiki*, 1983, no. 2:154–55.

Lobanov, N., and Povolotskii, E. "Tsel' issledovaniia—otnoshenie rabochikh k trudu." *S.T.*, 1984, no. 3:91–94.

Loznevaia, M. P., and Kheifets, L. S. "Nadbavka k dolzhnostnomu okladu." *EKO*, 1982, no. 2:116–23.

Luk'ianov, A. "Ekonomicheskoe i sotsiologicheskoe obespechenie organizatsii sorevnovaniia na kombinate." *S.T.*, 1982, no. 6:104–7.

Malein, N. S., et al., eds. *Sbornik normativnykh aktov po khoziaistvennomu zakonodatel'stvu*. Moscow, 1979.

Matthews, Mervyn. *Class and Society in Soviet Russia*. London: Allen Lane, 1972.

———. *Privilege in the Soviet Union*. London: Allen and Unwin, 1978.

———. *Soviet Sociology, 1964–75: A Bibliography*. New York: Praeger Publishers, 1978. In collaboration with T. Anthony Jones.

———. *Education in the Soviet Union*. London: Allen and Unwin, 1982.

———. *Poverty in the Soviet Union*. Cambridge, Engl.: Cambridge University Press, 1986.

Merson, A. "Kazhdomu spetsialistu—svoe mesto." *S.T.*, 1982, no. 9:96–101.

Mishchenko, V. T. "Kurs—na luchshee ispol'zovanie." *EKO*, 1982, no. 3:106–16.

Moskvichev, N. P. "Gorod, predpriiatiia i zhil'e." *EKO*, 1982, no. 7:171–79.

Nargizashvili, M. "Trydovaia aktivnost' molodezhi i reservy ee povysheniia." *S.T.*, 1982, no. 6:96–101.

Narodnoe khoziaistvo SSSR. Moscow (various years).

Narodnoe khoziaistvo SSSR za 70 let. Moscow, 1987.

Ovsiannikov, A. A. "Ratsionalizatsiia potrebleniia—tipologicheskii podkhod." *S.I.*, 1987, no. 4:65–70.

Pankin, M. "Sverkhurochnaia rabota." *S.T.*, 1982, no. 6:108–11.

Pchelintseva, G. A. "Zakreplenie spetsialistov v sel'skom khoziaistve." *S.I.*, 1985, no. 1:93–102.

Popova, I. M., and Moin, V. B. "Zarabotnaia plata kak sotsial'naia tsennost'." *S.I.*, 1983, no. 2:102–10.

Protasenko, T. Z. "Osnovnye kharakteristiki material'nogo blagosostoianiia (opyt vyborochnogo obsledovaniia)." *S.I.*, 1985, no. 3:101–10.

Radio Free Europe/Radio Liberty: Research Bulletin (English and Russian language series; cyclostyled). Munich.

Resheniia partii i pravitel'stva po khoziaistvennym voprosam. Vol. 11 onward. Moscow, 1977–.

Rimashevskaia, N. M. "Strukturnye izmeneniia v tendentsiiakh rosta blagosostoianiia." *S.I.*, 1985, no. 4:22–33.

Ruble, B. *Soviet Trade Unions*. Cambridge, Engl.: Cambridge University Press, 1981.

Rutgaizer, V. M. "Ratsional'noe ispol'zovanie obshchestvennykh fondov potrebleniia." *S.I.*, 1987, no. 2:139–40.

Rutgaizer, V. M., et al. "K voprosu o reforme sistemy potrebitel'skikh i denezhnykh dokhodov naseleniia." *Izvestiia Sibirskogo otdeleniia A. N. Seria ekonomika i prikladnaia sotsiologiia,* 1987, no. 13:41–51.

Rutgaizer, V. M.; Spivak, E. Iu.; and Shmarov, A. I. "Sotsial'no-regional'naia differentsiatsiia uslovii zhizni naseleniia." *S.I.,* 1987, no. 5:52–55.

Rutkevich, M. N. "O roli torgovli v sotsial'nom razviti sovetskogo obshchestva." *S.I.,* 1983, no. 1:16–28.

———. "Izmeneniia v sotsial'no-klassovi strukture sovetskogo obshchestva v usloviiakh perestroiki." *S.I.,* 1987, no. 5:34.

Ryvkina, R. V., and Fis'kova, L. K. "Vglub' sotsial'noi infrastruktury." *EKO,* 1982, no. 1:202–8.

Saksakulm, T. I. "Kak sdelat' trud bolee privlekatel'nym." *EKO,* 1982, no. 8: 49–52.

Sarkisian, G. "Strategiia uskoreniia i blagosostoianie naroda." *Voprosy ekonomiki,* 1987, no. 1:11–22.

Sarkisiants, G. "Sotsial'naia politika, trud i blagosostoianie." *S.T.,* 1986, no. 6:3–12.

Sbornik statisticheskikh materialov v pomoshch' agitatoru i propogandistu. Moscow, 1987.

Shirokalova, G. S. "K voprosu o pokazateliakh trudovoi aktivnosti." *S.I.,* 1985, no. 1:109–13.

Shirokova, L. N., and Mosina, L. L. "Raionnoe regulirovanie zarabotnoi platy." *EKO,* 1982, no. 2:105–16.

Shkaratan, O. I. "Effektivnost' truda i otnoshenie k trudu." *S.I.,* 1982, no. 1: 19–27.

Shmidt, V. I. "O stabilizatsii trudovykh kollektivov v usloviiakh vakhtovogo metoda organizatsii truda."*S.I.,* 1984, no. 1:55–59.

Shvetsov, Iu. G. "Sverkhurochnye raboty po initsiative trudashchikhsia." *S.I.,* 1985, no. 3:111–12.

Sidorova, M. "Sblizhenie urovnei zhizni gorodskogo i sel'skogo naseleniia." *Voprosy ekonomiki,* 1984, no. 9:53–62.

Simakov, A. G. "Zhil'e i zarplata v otsenke rabochykh." *EKO,* 1983, no. 7:105–8.

Solntsev, A. A. "Opyt issledovaniia otnosheniia k trudu rabotnikov torgovli." *S.I.,* 1984, no. 2:117–19.

Solov'ev, A. "Gotovitsia proekt novogo zakona o pensiiakh." *S.T.,* 1987, no. 4: 79–87.

Sosin, Iu. P. "Rabochee vremia: istochniki poter'." *EKO,* 1984, no. 10:156–62.

Spravochnik partiinogo rabotnika. Moscow (various years).

SSSR v tsifrakh v 1986. Moscow, 1987.

Stakanova, O. V. "Kvalifikatsionnye razlichiia i effektivnost' truda rabochikh." *S.I.,* 1984, no. 1:78–82.

Sukharev, A. Ia. (see *Iuridicheskii entsiklopedicheskii slovar'*).

Sverdlik, Sh. B. "Rost sberezhenii naseleniia: prichiny i sledstviia." *EKO,* 1982, no. 6:115–30.

Terebilov, V. I., ed. *Kommentarii k zakonodatel'stvu o trude.* Moscow, 1982.

Thierry, H., and Koopman-Iwema, A. M. "Motivation and Satisfaction." In P. J. D. Drench, et al., eds., *A Handbook of Work and Organisational Psychology.* Vol. 1. Chichester, Engl.: Wiley, 1984.

Tikhonov, A. M. "Ob usloviiakh truda i byta molodykh spetsialistov ugol'noi promyshlennosti USSR." *S.I.,* 1984, no. 2 : 114–15.

Tkachenko, A. A. "Otnoshenie k kachestvu produktsii." *EKO,* 1982, no. 8 : 35–41.

"Trudovye resursy regiona." *EKO,* 1982, no. 3 : 105–6.

U.S. Department of Commerce, Bureau of the Census. *Statistical Abstract of the United States.* Washington, D.C.: GPO (various years).

Vedomosti Verkhovnogo Soveta, no. 2, article 34, 1987.

Voeikov, M. I. "Sorevnovanie i sovershenstvovanie raspredeleniia po trudu." *S.I.,* 1984, no. 1 : 33–38.

Voronov, V. V., and Smirnov, I. P. "Zakreplenie molodezhi v zone BAMa." *S.I.,* 1982, no. 2 : 16–21.

Zdravomyslov, A. G.; Rozhin, V. P.; and Iadov, V. A. *Chelovek i ego rabota. Sotsiologicheskoe issledovanie.* Moscow, 1967.

Ziuzin, D. I. "Obshchestvennyi prizyv kak forma pereraspredeleniia trudovykh resursov." *S.I.,* 1985, no. 2 : 79–88.

Periodicals Used for Reference Purposes

Argumenty i fakty
Current Digest of the Soviet Press (CDSP; published in the USA)
EKO
Ekonomicheskaia gazeta
Ekonomika sel'skogo khoziaistva
Facts on File
Izvestiia
Izvestiia Sibirskogo otdeleniia Akademii Nauk SSSR
Keesing's Contemporary Archive
Literaturnaia gazeta
PlanEcon
Planovoe khoziaistvo
Pravda
Problems of Communism
Radio Liberty Research Bulletin (abbreviated as *R.L. Research Bulletin*)
Russkaia mysl' (Paris; also titled *La Pensée Russe*)
Sotsialisticheskii trud (abbreviated as *S.T.*)
Sotsial'noe obespechenie

Sotsiologicheskie issledovaniia (abbreviated as *S.I.*)
Soviet Economy
Trud
Vestnik statistiki
Voprosy ekonomiki
Zhurnalist

Index